101 FASCINATING Hockey FACTS

BRIAN McFARLANE

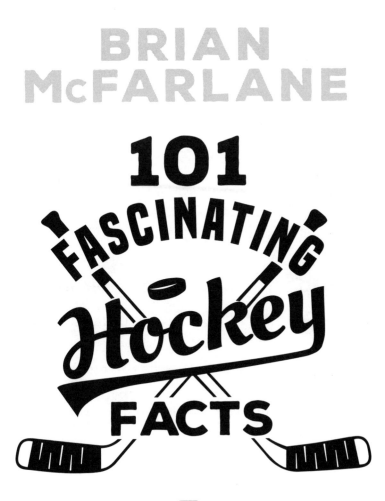

101 FASCINATING Hockey FACTS

DUNDURN
TORONTO

Publisher: Scott Fraser | Acquiring editor: Kathryn Lane | Editor: Allison Hirst
Cover designer: Laura Boyle
Printer: Webcom, a division of Marquis Book Printing Inc.

Library and Archives Canada Cataloguing in Publication

Title: 101 fascinating hockey facts / Brian McFarlane.
Other titles: One hundred one fascinating hockey facts | One hundred and one fascinating hockey facts
Names: McFarlane, Brian, author.
Identifiers: ISBN 9781459745667 (softcover) | ISBN 9781459745674 (PDF) | ISBN 9781459745681 (EPUB)
Subjects: LCSH: National Hockey League—Miscellanea. | LCSH: Hockey—Miscellanea.
Classification: LCC GV847.8.N3 M39 2019 | DDC 796.962/64—dc23

We acknowledge the support of the Canada Council for the Arts and the Ontario Arts Council for our publishing program. We also acknowledge the financial support of the Government of Ontario, through the Ontario Book Publishing Tax Credit and Ontario Creates, and the Government of Canada.

Printed and bound in Canada.

VISIT US AT

 dundurn.com | @dundurnpress | dundurnpress | dundurnpress

Dundurn
3 Church Street, Suite 500
Toronto, Ontario, Canada
M5E 1M2

To Anderson Whitehead, 12, and his hockey hero, Carey Price. Their emotional bonding in 2019 after Anderson's mother Laura McKay died from cancer at age 44 was a fascinating moment in hockey, one we'll long remember.

INTRODUCTION

Hockey has a fascinating history. And although Canada is the birthplace of the game, over the past century the sport has been adopted by countries all over the world. As a founding member of the Society for International Hockey Research, I'm one of many who diligently dig into hockey's past, and I am constantly surprised by the stories we uncover: Tales of triumph and tragedy, victory and defeat, camaraderie and conflict, and lots of crazy shenanigans, both on and off the ice.

Can you imagine a player scoring 14 goals in a single Stanley Cup game? Or leading his NHL team in scoring — with a mere 13 points? How about the NHL player who was still performing into his fifties — and a grandfather? How about the teenage goalie who travelled more than

4,000 miles to play for the Stanley Cup and allowed a record 32 goals in two Cup games?

I even created a little Stanley Cup lore myself by stepping on the ice with a microphone in the middle of a 1974 playoff game and earning a reprimand from the NHL president at the time. Still, it was a hockey "first."

The following pages contain a collection of 101 of these fascinating stories that occurred before and during my seven-decade-long career as a hockey broadcaster and writer. I hope you enjoy them!

THE STANLEY CUP THIEF

On April 2, 1962, during the Stanley Cup playoffs, a 25-year-old Montrealer saw his name and photo splashed across the sports pages of North America. Was it because he had won the Cup? No, it was because *he had stolen it!*

Ironically, the event happened on April Fool's Day. But it was no joke. At the Chicago Stadium, with the Blackhawks almost certain to win the semifinal series and the Cup, one diehard Canadiens fan named Ken Kilander sprang into action. Here is how he described what happened:

"In the '60s, I'd follow the Habs around all the time. I'd finance my road trips by playing piano in bars. I knew the Stanley Cup was locked up in a showcase in the lobby of the Chicago Stadium. So I said to some reporters, 'What would you fellows do if I went and got the Cup?'

"One of them laughed and said, 'Well, it *is* April Fool's Day. If you go and steal the Cup, I guarantee I'll put your picture in the paper.'

"So, when I saw my beloved Habs getting clobbered that night, I couldn't take any more of that. I ran down to the lobby and I pushed in on this glass showcase and the lock gave way.

"I grabbed the Cup and walked away fast…. An usher spotted me and started yelling, 'Stop him! Help! Some guy's stealing the Cup!' His screams brought some policemen running and they arrested me. It's hard to run fast when you're lugging the Stanley Cup.

"The next morning I appeared before a judge, who took pity on me. He said, 'You can go back to the Stadium tomorrow night and cheer for your Canadiens. But the Cup stays here unless the Blackhawks lose, which they will not.' Then he smiled at me and let me go.

"The judge was right. Chicago won the series, but lost to Toronto in the Cup finals. And I was lucky not to be fined or thrown in jail."

LAFLEUR ALSO A CUP THIEF

Ken Kilander isn't the only Montrealer who stole the Stanley Cup. After the Canadiens won the Cup in 1979, there was, of course, a team victory party — actually, several victory parties. At one of them, Guy Lafleur, the team's top scorer with 52 goals, slipped the Stanley Cup into the trunk of his car and drove away with it. Nobody had seen him leave, and soon there were cries of, "Where's the Cup? It's gone missing. Who stole the Stanley Cup?"

Only Guy Lafleur knew. And he was taking it for a little ride, all the way to the home of his parents in Thurso, Quebec.

Rejean Lafleur, Guy's father, was surprised and excited when Guy arrived. Together, they placed the Cup on the front lawn. Word travelled fast in the small community, and people came running — all of them with cameras. They came from miles around, once word spread that the Cup was sitting on Rejean Lafleur's lawn.

Hundreds of people lined up to have their photos taken with it. And with Guy.

By then, Guy was beginning to feel guilty. On the radio he heard that Montreal fans — and the custodians of the Cup — were alarmed because the Stanley Cup had gone missing, and a search for it was under way.

"I'd better get the Cup back to Montreal, where it belongs," he told his parents.

So he loaded up the trophy and rushed back to the Canadiens' front office. He hurried in carrying the Cup and left it with a receptionist. When asked for an explanation, he said, "Sorry, I'm in a big hurry." He ran out and raced off. No doubt he had a big smile on his face all the way back to Thurso.

KIDNAPPING ESPO

In the spring of 1973, the Boston Bruins were eliminated from the Stanley Cup playoffs by the New York Rangers. During the series, Bruins star Phil Esposito was hospitalized in Boston with a leg injury. When the Boston players decided to hold their post-season party, they agreed that Esposito must attend, bad leg and all. They decided to kidnap their leader from the hospital — for just a few hours.

While two of the Bruins distracted the nurses on duty, other players wheeled Esposito — still in his hospital bed — into an elevator and out a side exit. Somehow a door with a glass window was broken during the escape.

The Bruins guided the hospital bed and its famous patient down the avenue while drivers beeped their horns as they drove past. Led by Wayne Cashman and Bobby Orr, the players wheeled Esposito around a corner to their favourite restaurant — the Branding Iron.

When the Bruins were partied out, they wheeled Esposito back to the hospital — a bumpy ride because one of the bed's wheels had loosened — where they were confronted by hospital officials, who were not amused by their prank. One of them presented the Bruins with an invoice listing several hundred dollars' worth of "damages to hospital property." While Espo slept, so the story goes, his mates slipped the invoice into the pocket of his pyjamas.

Recently, in Naples, Florida, I met two retired doctors. Both had been young men on duty that night at the Boston hospital. They both chuckled when they recalled all the commotion caused by Bobby Orr and the Bruins.

Dr. Tucker Aufranc, a former orthopedic surgeon, remembers the difficulty the Bruins players had at one point. "They chose a small elevator and had to tilt Phil's bed up to get it inside. So either his head was almost on the floor or his feet were. It was a tight fit. When they broke a glass door in their haste, some hospital officials came running. But too late to stop them."

AN OFF-ICE PUNCH-UP

George McPhee, general manager of the Washington Capitals, became furious when the Chicago Blackhawks played "too many aggressive players" during a pre-season game. Following the match, he confronted Chicago coach Lorne Molleken, lost his temper, and punched him in the head. In response, Hawks players jumped McPhee, leaving him with a torn suit and missing his watch.

NHL commissioner Gary Bettman suspended McPhee for a month without pay and fined him $20,000. His confrontation with Molleken "started in a civil manner," McPhee said, "but got a bit out of hand."

No, George, more than a bit.

Bill Wirtz, the Chicago Blackhawks' owner, then 70 years old, was fined $3,000 for suggesting, "Let's lock the top brass of both teams in a room, turn out the lights, and start swinging away. That'll settle things."

Off-ice confrontations are not unusual. In the mid-1980s, several New York Rangers objected to large mugs of beer being thrown onto their bench by drunken fans at Detroit's Joe Louis Arena. So they chased spectators up the stairs, swinging sticks and dulling their skate blades on the cement steps.

When defenceman Mike Milbury was playing for the Boston Bruins, he and his mates rushed into the stands at Madison Square Garden during a game to fight with Rangers fans. Milbury was seen whacking one fellow on the head with his own shoe. And there was a memorable scene in the 1988 playoffs when New Jersey Devils coach Jim Schoenfeld, after a loss to the Bruins, confronted burly referee Don Koharski in a corridor of the arena and screamed at him, "Have another doughnut, you fat pig!" after disagreeing with the official's calls.

When other NHL officials refused to work the following game in New Jersey, citing the incident, the league hastily recruited three amateurs. League president John Ziegler could not be consulted for an opinion because he could not be found. All in all, it was a bad day for the NHL, though a memorable one.

THE GREATEST DETRIMENT TO HOCKEY

When he wasn't sitting in the penalty box, he was sitting in a bar. Or in jail. When he wasn't drunk, he was about to get drunk. He was handsome, witty, and charming. Women couldn't resist him. His name was Howie Young, and he was a Red Wings defenceman in the 1960s.

Young regularly broke team curfews and the law. He drove his coaches and manager crazy. NHL president Clarence Campbell once said, "He's the greatest detriment to hockey that has ever laced on skates."

Old-timers like me have lingering images of Young's bizarre actions. One night he showed up for a game wearing a Beatles wig. He once spat at Maple Leafs owner Stafford Smythe. While a Red Wing, he assaulted a cop during a Memorial Cup game and the officer was carried out on a stretcher, concussed.

His friends say it's amazing he played as long and as well as he did, considering the vast quantities of booze he consumed, measured in barrels, not bottles. "Yeah, about 12 foggy years," he told me one night in a Montreal bar (he was drinking Diet Coke). "Always into the sauce, always hungover. That's what I did for a dozen years. And yet, I was one of a few hockey players to make the cover of *Sports Illustrated*."

Between 1960 and 1968, the tough defenceman played five seasons with Gordie Howe and the Red Wings. The fans loved him, and he once finished just behind Howe in a popularity poll.

But he was less popular with his teammates. One year they lobbied to keep him out of the playoffs because they felt he hurt their chances of winning the Stanley Cup.

When Detroit manager Jack Adams had seen enough, he dealt Young to Chicago. There were a few games with the Vancouver Canucks, followed by some minor-league stops, including a final stint — a comeback — with Flint in some obscure league when he was 48 years old.

At one time during the '60s, he palled around with Frank Sinatra. Old Blue Eyes even got him a bit part in one of the crooner's movies. Young displayed his thanks by throwing Sinatra off a yacht into the ocean. After Sinatra's bodyguards hauled their boss back on deck, they found a sandy beach and roughly deposited Young onto it.

After his hockey days, somehow Young pulled himself together, wised up, and stayed on the wagon for the rest of his life, working as a cowboy and a truck driver.

He went missing for years until writer George Gamester of the *Toronto Star* caught up with him in tiny Thoreau, New Mexico, where the former NHLer was driving a school bus. He'd been sober for 33 years. He had a wife named China, a horse, a dozen cats, and some dogs. "I'm so happy here," he told Gamester. He talked about raising money to build a hockey rink "so the kids here can enjoy the game like I did."

Sadly, within a few months, on November 24, 1999, Howie Young was dead of pancreatic cancer at the age of 62.

ONE LUCKY GUY

During the 1980s and '90s, Pat Verbeek was one of the NHL's best right wingers. He was also a very lucky guy.

In the summer of 1985, Verbeek's career appeared to be over when, while working on his farm near Forest, Ontario, his left thumb was severed when he caught his hand in a corn-planting machine.

The thumb had dropped into a load of fertilizer, and while Pat was rushed to hospital in nearby Sarnia, his parents searched frantically for the missing digit. They finally located it, packed it in ice, and drove it to the hospital, where it was reattached. One of the surgeons was not optimistic. "Your hockey career may be over, son," he said. "A hockey player can't grip his stick without a healthy thumb."

But soon, circulation returned to the thumb, and Verbeek began lifting weights and squeezing grips to strengthen his hand. When a new season got under way, he quipped, "I think the thumb has even grown a bit. Because of all that fertilizer it fell in."

Pat made an amazing recovery. Fifteen years later he was scoring goals at a Hall of Fame pace. In 2000–2001, as a member of the Stanley Cup–winning Dallas Stars, he joined 27 other NHLers in the 500-goal club. He finished his career with 522 goals and 1,067 points. Those sound like Hall of Fame numbers to me!

ACE BAILEY, NOT SO LUCKY

One of the most famous dates in history is 9/11/01. On that date, September 11, 2001, terrorists commandeered passenger jets and flew them into the World Trade Center in New York City.

Former NHL hockey player Garnet "Ace" Bailey, director of pro scouting for the Los Angeles Kings, was late getting to Logan Airport in Boston that day. But he arrived just in time to board his flight — United Airlines Flight 175, en route to Los Angeles. Shortly after takeoff, the plane was hijacked by terrorists and diverted to New York City, where it crashed into the south tower of the World Trade Center. All on board were killed and the tower destroyed. Bailey, 53, a member of two Stanley Cup–winning teams with Boston in 1970 and 1972, and a scout for the Edmonton Oilers for

13 years during the '80s when the team won five Stanley Cups, is remembered as a popular player and a mentor to Wayne Gretzky when he first joined the NHL.

Hockey writer Kevin Dupont (*Boston Globe*) wrote about widow Kathy Bailey's courage as she dealt with the loss of a husband and father. "I'm in a place where I know I'll truly never get over what happened. Nothing can change that day."

Ten years after her loss, Kathy Bailey was back at Logan, dropping off relatives who were heading off on vacation. It was a United flight. For the first time since that fateful day, she found herself at the very spot where she last said goodbye to the man she had married in 1972.

Then she looked behind the check-in counter just as a Los Angeles Kings hockey bag moved along the conveyor belt.

Her sister-in-law, Paula, saw her reaction and said, "Oh, Kathy, does that upset you?" Kathy smiled and said, "No, I'm fine ... that was just Ace saying hello."

BELISLE, GET HALF-DRESSED!

In 1960, forward Danny Belisle was playing for Vancouver in the Western Hockey League when he was called up to the New York Rangers on Christmas Day. The rookie's first game was against the Montreal Canadiens, the best team in hockey at the time and winners of a record five straight Stanley Cups. "The Rangers were a sixth-place team headed for the Dumpster," Danny told me.

Belisle scored a goal in that game and added another over the next three. Before the fifth game, he was in the Rangers locker room, putting on his gear and feeling pleased with himself. He was off to a good start. He'd been called up because Camille Henry was injured and a doubtful starter. Danny had most of his equipment on when coach Alf Pike came into the room, took him aside, and said, "Hey, kid, take your gear off. I think Camille Henry is ready to go."

Danny was disappointed but shrugged and began taking off his equipment. A few minutes later, Pike came back and told Danny, "Kid, put your gear back on. We're not sure Henry can play after all."

So Danny began putting his equipment back on, not saying a word because rookies didn't utter a peep in those days. About five minutes later, Pike was back. "Hey, kid, we're still not sure about Henry. I want you to get half-dressed."

Half-dressed? At this point Danny felt a bit foolish, getting dressed and then undressed and dressed again. Was this all a practical joke? So he put the bottom part of his equipment on: jock, shin pads, hockey pants. Then, impishly, he donned his shoes, his shirt and tie, and his suit jacket. His teammates looked over and suddenly began to laugh. "I was standing there half-dressed, like I'd been told," he said. "But the dressing room was in hysterics. And just then, Coach Pike came trotting back in. He stood and gawked at me. I said, 'Hey, coach, I'm half-dressed like you said.' And he says, 'Yeah, well, take everything off. Camille Henry is ready to play.' I didn't know it then, but I'd played my last game in the National Hockey League. I was sent back to the minors the following day. Never got another chance."

LITTLE LEAGUER TO BIG LEAGUER

When 12-year-old Chris Drury and his Little League base-ball teammates from Trumbull, Connecticut, showed up at the ballpark in Williamsport, New York, one afternoon in 1989, they were astonished to find more than 40,000 base-ball fans waiting for them. The throng had arrived early, anxious to see the final game of the 1989 Little League World Series, which normally attracts about 25,000 fans.

Drury, the Trumbull team's starting pitcher, knew that the kids from Taiwan — the opposing team — were out-standing. They'd beaten the best U.S. teams three years run-ning and had outscored them 43–1.

The Taiwanese batters expected fastballs from Chris but found themselves waving feebly at his junk balls. Chris won the game with his "loopers" by a 5–2 score and became a national hero.

Later, he'd become even more famous on the hockey rink.

While attending Boston University, there was a National Collegiate Athletic Association (NCAA) title for Chris as well as a Hobey Baker Award as the top college player in the nation. Chris is the only player to score more than 100 career goals and 100 assists for Boston U.

As a pro, he broke in with the Colorado Avalanche in the NHL and captured the Calder Trophy as rookie of the year. In the 2000–2001 season, he established himself as a clutch goal scorer as Colorado marched all the way to the Stanley Cup.

Chris went on to play for Calgary and Buffalo before signing with the Rangers in 2007, lured by a contract worth $35.25 million over five years. He became the Rangers' captain and, following his retirement after 892 NHL games, the team's assistant general manager.

TARO! TARO! TARO!

The NHL entry draft of 1974 was conducted in secret, with all the choices being made over the telephone. The hush-hush draft was held behind closed doors because of increasing competition for young players by the competing World Hockey Association (WHA).

The Buffalo Sabres contributed the most amusing twist to the event. In the 12th round of the draft, GM Punch Imlach selected an unknown Japanese star, Taro Tsujimoto. Tsujimoto was described as a five-foot-eight, 180-pound centre from the Tokyo Katanas. It marked the first time an Asian player had been drafted into the NHL.

Weeks later, when Tsujimoto failed to show up for training camp, Imlach confessed it was all a joke. He'd plucked Tsujimoto's name from the Buffalo telephone book, and no such hockey player existed. "I just wanted to add a little fun to those dreary draft proceedings," Imlach said, chuckling. To his surprise, his hoax didn't fade and die. Years later, Buffalo fans were still flashing signs at Sabres' games: "WE WANT TARO."

Imlach and the Sabres made a much smarter choice at the 1983 draft. A teenage goalie named Tom Barrasso was a star for the Acton-Boxborough high school team in Massachusetts with a record of 22-0-1. The Sabres took a gamble. Punch Imlach drafted him fifth overall, unusually high for an amateur goalie. Some so-called experts scoffed at the choice, but Barrasso, just 18 years old, went straight from high school to the Sabres and skated off with the Calder Trophy as top rookie, and the Vezina Trophy as top goalie. No minor-league mentoring for him. It was astonishing to see an unknown teen outperform all the more famous names in NHL netminding.

Barrasso went on to win 369 NHL games and two Stanley Cups (with Pittsburgh) over his career. He also holds the NHL record for points by a goalie with 48 — all assists. Here are the top four point-scoring goalies. Barrasso is in good company.

Goalie	Seasons	Points
Tom Barrasso	19	48
Martin Brodeur	22	47
Grant Fuhr	19	47
Patrick Roy	19	45

THE MOST FEARED MAN IN THE EASTERN HOCKEY LEAGUE

John Brophy was the terror of the old Eastern Hockey League. Some even say he was the biggest villain in the history of hockey.

One night, in the decrepit Cherry Hill Arena in New Jersey, Brophy's Long Island Ducks defeated the home team in a playoff series. After that final game, Brophy stood at centre ice and blew kisses to the seething fans, who hurled everything at him: programs, beer cans, bottles. The debris piled up, and Brophy fell to his knees and blew more kisses. He stopped and backed away only when a toilet seat came flying down at him. Perhaps he thought the toilet would follow — or a bathtub. With a final salute, he made a dash for his team's dressing room.

When Brophy and the equally pugnacious Don Perry teamed up on defence for the Long Island Ducks, they were masters of intimidation.

Playing at home against the New Haven Blades one night, they clobbered two or three of the visitors on their very first shift. That was enough. The Blades fled the ice, put on their street clothes, and went home. They even turned down an offer of a hundred bucks per player to stay.

The game lasted all of 80 seconds.

As a coach, John Brophy ranks second only to Scotty Bowman in wins, most of them in the minors. Brophy hated losing. After one loss, he pulled a Rolex off his wrist, placed it on the floor, and smashed it to smithereens. He took off his suit jacket and tore it to shreds. He sat at the front of the team bus, and as it pulled away, he punched a hole in the side window. The bus driver told him, "If you ever do that again, you're barred from my bus." Brophy glared at the driver and said, "Buddy, if you say another word, I'm gonna kick you off and drive the fucking bus myself."

Another time, after another loss, Brophy was just as livid. He smashed his team's weight machine to pieces, ripped the stick holder off the wall, and broke every stick the team owned.

Gregg Inkpen, Brophy's biographer, says that Brophy is the only coach he is aware of who ever stole the keys to a minor-league rink's Zamboni. And the reason he did it: He apparently didn't want his opponents to have a fresh sheet of ice to skate on!

Brophy died in Antigonish, Nova Scotia, in 2017, at the age of 83.

DON'T YOU DARE MENTION HIS NAME!

Right winger Bill Flett was traded from the Los Angeles Kings to the Philadelphia Flyers, where he played a big role in two consecutive Stanley Cup wins, in 1974 and '75. (I covered those series for NBC back then and saw the Flyers — the Broad Street Bullies — at their best and worst.)

On his first trip back to play the Kings at the Great Western Forum, Flett scored a pure hat trick — three straight goals. He also earned an assist and was the obvious choice to be named star of the game. But not only was he not named the number one star, he was overlooked for star number two and star number three.

How come? you ask.

Well, Jack Kent Cooke, the Kings' owner, was so angered by Flett's performance that he rushed down to the rinkside announcer's booth and pointed at the man with the microphone. "Don't you dare mention Flett's name," he barked.

"But, Mr. Cooke, he scored four points."

"Never mind. You heard me. You mention his name over that microphone and you're fired!"

It took some scrambling to find another star, and Flett's dazzling performance went unrecognized.

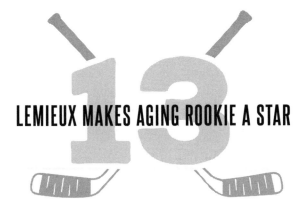

LEMIEUX MAKES AGING ROOKIE A STAR

From 1980 through 1984, Warren Young was an unsung, unappreciated, unhappy hockey player riding the hockey buses through minor-league cities. His career was going nowhere, his NHL chances fading fast. When he was invited to Pittsburgh's training camp prior to the 1984–85 season, he was 28, nearly a has-been by NHL standards. But somehow he clicked on a line with 19-year-old rookie sensation Mario Lemieux. The two fit together like (Brett) Hull and (Adam) Oates, and Young became a big-league celebrity overnight. Thanks to Mario's passes, Young finished the season with 40 goals. He added 32 assists and won a berth on the rookie all-star squad.

The following season, the Detroit Red Wings went on a spending spree, throwing millions at free agents. Young signed a multi-year contract with the Wings that had him earning twice as much as Lemieux's base salary of $125,000. But without Lemieux to set him up, Young's goal production dropped dramatically, and he soon faded from the hockey scene.

Young retired in 1988 after playing 236 games in the NHL and scoring 72 goals. Five years later, he played four games with the Pittsburgh Phantoms in a little-known roller hockey league.

THE AMAZING MULLENS

The Mullen brothers, Brian and Joey, grew up in a rough area of New York City called Hell's Kitchen. They were almost in their teens before they learned how to skate. The hockey they had enjoyed up to that point was played on asphalt and cement — roller hockey. But the brothers were lucky. Their father, Tom Mullen, had a job at Madison Square Garden, where the Mullen boys got to skate from time to time. They collected broken and battered sticks from the New York Rangers players they met. They even dreamed of someday leading the Rangers to the Stanley Cup. Nobody gave them one chance in a million of ever doing that.

But somehow they acquired the skills that would take them to college hockey and then on to the highest level in the game. Joey would never make it, he was often told. Having branded him as too small and too slow, the big-league scouts simply shrugged when his name was mentioned. He was ignored by all but one NHL club. Eventually, Joey signed on as a free agent with the St. Louis Blues and played with their minor-league club. It was his chance to prove that all the scouts had been wrong about him, and when he got his NHL chance, he played far above anyone's expectations.

In the next 17 years, Joey Mullen scored 502 career goals in the NHL, the most by any U.S.-born player up to that time. He averaged a point a game in 1,062 games with five different clubs and played a key role on three Stanley Cup winners — with Calgary in 1989 and Pittsburgh in 1991 and 1992. He also captured two Lady Byng trophies as hockey's most gentlemanly player.

Not bad for a kid who was too small, too slow, and too late getting started in hockey to amount to anything.

In November 2000, Mullen added another ring to his collection — this one signifying his induction into the Hockey Hall of Fame.

What about Brian Mullen? you ask. He, too, went from roller hockey and a job as a stick boy to a college career at Wisconsin. He was signed by the Winnipeg Jets in 1982 and played on a line with star centre Dale Hawerchuk for five seasons, consistently scoring between 20 and 30 goals a season. Between 1982 and 1992, he played with the Jets, the Rangers, the Sharks, and the Islanders. His biggest playoff thrill was helping the Islanders dethrone the two-time champion Pittsburgh Penguins in 1993. The series went seven games before the Islanders completed the upset with a win in overtime.

In 1993, Brian suffered a small stroke, caused by a hole in his heart through which a blood clot had moved upward, threatening his brain. After some delicate surgery, he was back on skates. But a year later, he suffered another seizure, and doctors told him his hockey career was over.

A MILLION FOR MIRO

was general manager of the Leafs (1982–1988), he acquired a solid Czech player, Peter Ihnacak. When McNamara heard that Ihnacak had a younger brother named Miroslav, who was reputed to be a scoring star back home, he got goosebumps. He even had Darryl Sittler's number 27 waiting for his new recruit.

Miro Ihnacak had never been scouted by the Leafs. No one in the organization had even seen what he looked like. But the Leafs arranged for Ihnacak's defection from Czechoslovakia. It was rumoured that young Miro was an awesome physical specimen — six foot two and close to 200 pounds.

When he finally stepped on the ice at Maple Leaf Gardens to display his skills, onlookers were shocked. He was a lightweight, and no taller than five eleven. And his skating, stickhandling, and shooting skills were no better than average.

It didn't take the media long to get on his case. His nickname soon became Miro the Zero, and in 56 games as a Leaf, he scored just eight goals.

He proved to be one of the most expensive flops in hockey history, costing the Toronto club close to a million dollars in fees, salary, and expenses to spirit him out of his native land and give him an all-too-brief taste of life in the NHL.

The Red Wings gave Ihnacak a one-game look, and then — surprise — he finally blossomed in the American Hockey League (AHL), scoring 115 goals over three seasons.

PUT A SOCK IN IT, EDDIE!

If Eddie Shack had kept his trap shut, he might have been on two Boston Stanley Cup winners — one in 1970 and a second one in 1972. But Shack was dumped by the Bruins, traded to the L.A. Kings before Boston captured those two Cups. And the reason behind the trade is laughable. Shack claims it's because he made fun of the owner's hats.

"I used to sell Biltmore hats all around the league. Remember the beauties Punch Imlach wore when I was with the Leafs? He bought 'em from me. But the Boston owner, Weston Adams, a millionaire and a cheap son of a bitch, wouldn't buy any of my hats. He wore the oldest, crappiest hats in the world. And I let him know it. That's when he said, 'Nice knowin' you, Eddie.' I'm sure he told the manager to get rid of me, and I was traded to the Kings. Nobody wore hats out there.

"So that's why I missed out on two more Stanley Cup rings to go with the four I won with the Leafs."

Shack is one of two players to score 20 or more goals in a season for five or more NHL teams. (Bill Guerin is the other, notching 20 goals for seven different teams.)

Former Buffalo Sabre Mike Byers recalls playing on a line with Eddie in Buffalo. "We were waiting for the faceoff in the other team's zone, and just before the official dropped the puck, Shack yells, 'Hold on a minute!' We all look over at him and he's taking his hockey stick, turning it around, and cocking it like a rifle. Then he put the stick back in its original position and nodded, indicating he was ready for the faceoff.

"Wouldn't you know, when the puck was dropped, it came right back to Shack and he snapped it into the net for a goal. Later I heard him tell reporters he'd stopped the game because his 'gun' was out of bullets. I'll say this: He picked a great time to reload."

ARTIFICIAL ICE CAME EARLY

London, England, was the first home of artificial ice. In December 1841, chemically made ice was invented and covered a tiny surface of 12 by 6 feet. It was used for skating only, and it was hardly a rink: more a rinky-dink rink.

In January 1876, another small artificial ice rink — the Glaciarium — opened for skating in Chelsea, England. Professor John Gamgee developed a process of flooding the floor of the rink with water poured over flattened copper pipes. A combination of ether, glycerine, and water was then pumped through the pipes, producing intense cold in the pipes, which froze the water poured on top. The Glaciarium was a smelly place. Music for the skaters was supplied by a small orchestra.

In 1877, a second rink was opened nearby, with dressing rooms for ladies. Smoking was allowed at one end of the rink but not the other. The first game of curling on artificial ice was played there.

The first mechanically refrigerated ice rink constructed in the United States was installed by engineer Thomas Rankin in 1879, at the Old Madison Square Garden in New York City. Rankin was saluted at a gala skating carnival held on the night of February 12, 1879, and was thrilled to see hundreds of masked skaters, dressed in fancy costumes, circling the famous arena on his slick new ice while thousands of spectators watched from the stands.

By 1896, Baltimore had an artificial ice arena, and on December 26, a game featuring seven-per-side hockey was played between a team from Johns Hopkins University and some players from the Baltimore Athletic Club. This may have been the first game of ice hockey played on a sheet of artificial ice, and it was one of the first games played in the United States. The game lasted 60 minutes, with an intermission after 30 minutes. About 2,500 curious spectators attended.

WANNA SKATE? MEET ME IN ST. LOUIS

In 1876, St. Louis boasted the largest man-made skating rink in the world. For skaters only, the Olive Street Rink — a gigantic sheet of natural ice measuring 450 feet by 500 feet, with a pavilion and a band — was quite spectacular, but it closed after one season. A period of temperatures above freezing was probably the reason.

According to hockey historian Darin Wernig, an artificial rink was built in St. Louis in 1899. Shortly after the Ice Palace opened, a six-team hockey league was formed. The ice surface was 168 feet by 110 feet. A team of transplanted Canadians (the All Canadians) won the championship in the first season of play.

GET THAT REF!

In the early days of the game, referees took plenty of blame and abuse. In an 1895 game played in Quebec City, Ottawa edged Quebec 3–2 and the crowd blamed the loss on the referee, a man named Hamilton. After the game, Hamilton ran toward the railway station, hoping to catch the midnight train back to Montreal. But a number of fans set off in pursuit, caught up to him, and dragged him back to the arena, where they tried to coerce him into declaring the match a draw. Police arrived just in time to rescue the shaken official and escort him back to the train station. They made sure he was able to flee the city without being tarred and feathered.

In 1899, referee Jim Findlay caused an uproar in a Stanley Cup game between Montreal and a challenging team from Winnipeg. Montreal player Bob McDougall whacked

Winnipeg star Tony Gingras with his stick and Gingras was carried off the ice. Findlay gave McDougall a two-minute penalty. "Not enough!" screamed the Winnipeg players. "Throw him out! We won't play until you do." They proceeded to skate off the ice to sulk in their dressing room.

Referee Findlay shrugged, removed his skates, and left for home in a horse-drawn sleigh. Officials chased after him and persuaded him to return. But an hour had passed, and the players and fans had scattered, possibly to a nearby tavern, and the game was never finished.

Fans in Quebec City went after another referee a season or two after they'd chased referee Hamilton. Billy Nicholson, captain of the Montreal Shamrocks, was refereeing a game between Quebec City and the Montreal Wanderers one night when irate fans assaulted him and tore his suit to pieces. Nicholson presented a bill to the league for damages to his clothing — the amount: $15. The Quebec City team paid it.

Some referees were more opinionated than others. On January 8, 1903, Mr. Fred Waghorne, the famous referee who introduced the whistle to stop play (in place of a cowbell), once refereed a game in the small town of Stouffville, Ontario. He told a sports reporter: "I want no more work in tiny rinks. I will, in the future, decline to officiate in hockey games where the ice surface is no larger than an English billiard table."

MELEE IN MONTREAL

Shortly after the turn of the 20th century, there was wild excitement in Montreal over a Stanley Cup playoff game against the visitors from Ottawa. When 4,000 fans outside the arena couldn't wait for the doors to open, hundreds made a mad rush into the building, smashing in the doors, breaking some windows, and streaming into the arena.

The melee started when enthusiastic fans found the centre doors locked. They proceeded to break in the panels. Not a board was left in the two big circular panels, each about two feet in diameter. Half a dozen venturesome souls climbed the porch and crawled over the big electric sign at the risk of losing their lives. They smashed in the windows. Another group unearthed a ladder and climbed their way to the upper promenade, entering through the broken windows.

Inside the rink, hundreds battled for space at the heads of the aisles, where they were lined up seven and eight deep. The steel girders held their usual quota of daring fans, with some young lads climbing up and onto the rafters over the ice. The match had already started when a group of 25 or so, who had lined up for the final allotment of standing-room tickets, rushed the door and swept everything aside — policemen, ushers, doors, and gates. The wife of a prominent arena official lost her skirt in a rush to the entrance. Several ladies were in a state of collapse when they finally got into the arena. Dresses were torn and fur garments were scattered all around.

It was impossible for officials to evict all the invaders, so the game was played before a full house, even though many of the spectators were freeloaders.

SOME DANDY NEW RULES

At the turn of the 19th century, a number of Ottawa fans called for some changes to the rules of the game. One hockey executive, T. Emmett Quinn, president of the Ottawa club, decided to take them seriously. After some deep thought at the next league meeting, Quinn proposed the following rule changes:

1. The puck should be painted green and reduced to half its present size, thus making it more difficult for goaltenders to see and to stop.

2. Players should be compelled to carry enough bills in their pockets to pay any fines they may receive on the spot.

3. Instead of giving a player a minor penalty, the referee should stop the play, take the offender

to the side boards, and have an earnest discussion with him for half a minute so that he might reform him.

Mr. Quinn thought the proposed changes, if adopted, would be popular and good for the game. But his colleagues disagreed and voted them down.

A SINGLE COIN MADE THEM PROS

In 1902, Jack Gibson's amateur team won a league championship in Berlin (now Kitchener), Ontario. Each player was awarded a single gold coin for the triumph. But the Ontario Hockey Association (OHA) stepped in and banned the players from further play because the gift of a coin made them professionals. Their offer to return the coins was refused.

Gibson's response was to form a team of professional players in 1902, based in Houghton, Michigan, where he'd set up a dental practice.

By 1904, Gibson had recruited several of the best players in the world to perform before as many as 5,000 fans in hockey's first professional league — the International Professional Hockey League (IPHL). In addition to the Houghton-Portage

Lakes, the Calumet Miners, the Michigan Soo Indians, the Pittsburgh Pro Hockey Club, and the Canadian Soo team rounded out the league.

The Houghton-Portage Lakes played at a new arena — the Amphidrome on Portage Lake. The Calumet Miners played at the Palestra (Michigan). Sault Ste. Marie (Michigan) and Sault Ste. Marie (Ontario) played at their local curling rinks — tiny surfaces on which to play a hockey game.

The league attracted some of the best players from Canada, men who received $15 to $40 a week to play while holding lucrative jobs in the community. Ottawa's Hod Stuart was paid $1,800 for the season by the Calumet club. He played for the Miners and also managed the rink he played in. Cyclone Taylor was the highest-paid player, signed to a salary of more than $3,000.

Because teams played on natural ice, the season ended after about two months. Most of the players left for their Canadian homes and their regular jobs at the conclusion. Calumet won the first league championship in 1905. In 1906 and 1907, Houghton took the honours.

The league folded after only three seasons, when professional hockey finally became a reality in Canada in 1907. Fifteen of the 97 players who played in the IPHL from 1904 to 1907, including Gibson, are honoured members of the Hockey Hall of Fame.

ONE CRAZY SERIES

A puck in the rafters, a dog on the ice, half a puck, and players in gold gowns, not to mention the player who "killed" himself.

One of my favourite Stanley Cup stories includes all of the above. It happened in Winnipeg back in 1902, in a best-of-three series between the Winnipeg Vics and the Toronto Wellingtons.

Fans came from miles around to jam into the 3,000-seat arena to witness the first Stanley Cup matches played in Manitoba. The Winnipeg Vics skated onto the ice for the warm-up wearing long gold dressing gowns over their uniforms. The referee had a little chat with both teams prior to dropping the puck. While he talked, snow fell through cracks in the roof and formed lines on the ice.

Midway through the first game, one of the "lifters" — a player noted for his ability to hoist the puck down the ice — hurled it high over the players' heads. But it did not come down! It had gotten lodged among the rink rafters. The players milled about and hurled their sticks up while the spectators laughed and cheered. The player whose stick finally dislodged the puck received quite an ovation.

There was then another long delay when a Newfoundland dog jumped onto the ice, resulting in a merry chase.

A reporter also wrote about a most unusual goal that was scored: "In a scrimmage near the Vics' goal, the puck was broken cleanly in two. [Toronto's] 'Chummy' Hill grabbed one piece and sailed in and shot for a goal. Referee McFarlane was forced to make a quick decision and he allowed the goal to stand."

It remains the only Stanley Cup series in history in which a goal was scored with half a puck.

A recurring phrase in a newspaper account of the game catches the eye: "Gingras was sent to the fence." Later in the summary, it appears again. "Gingras was told once again to sit on the fence." Finally, it becomes obvious. There was no penalty box for naughty Gingras to sit in. They hadn't been invented yet. Gingras simply sat on the low boards until the referee told him he could play again.

There was another playoff first during the game, when the puck sailed over the boards into the crowd. Normally, the spectator catching the puck would return it promptly to the ice. But the fan broke with tradition by pocketing the puck and refusing to give up his souvenir. Finally, another puck was sent for and the game continued.

One reporter wrote about the play of one of the Wellington players: "McKay tried to do too much work and killed himself. In the first half he was the life of the team, but several hard body checks put him out of business and he had to retire. He came on again after a rest, but could not stand the pace and fell on the ice. He had to be removed to the dressing room."

Winnipeg won the series in two straight games and entertained the Wellingtons at a reception following the victory. The Stanley Cup was fetched from a jewellery store window, where it had been on display, and was presented to the winners.

The Winnipeg papers were filled with lengthy descriptions of the play and quotes from the men involved. The Cup victory was front-page news, the game coverage eye-popping. There were neat little pen-and-ink illustrations of the game, including one of Gingras sitting on the fence.

Back home in Toronto, one of the Wellingtons cried when he heard about all the excitement he had missed. His parents had refused to let him go on the trip to Winnipeg, stating he was far too young for such gallivanting.

GETTING CHARLIE TO THE GAME

Early in 1902, a Montreal team left by train for Ottawa to play a big game against the Senators. But Charlie Liffiton, Montreal's star player, was not on board. He had a full-time job and fumed in frustration when his boss would not let him off work early. "Leave to play hockey, Charlie?" he had said. "Forget it. Stay at your desk." So Charlie missed the train.

Montreal team officials huddled and agreed their chances against Ottawa were slim without their best player. So they chartered a special train, with a single passenger aboard — Charlie Liffiton. The engineer and fireman pushed the train to breakneck speeds, and the train arrived in Ottawa a few minutes before game time. A horse-drawn sleigh delivered Liffiton to the arena in time to throw on his uniform and take the opening faceoff. Team officials paid $114 to the Canadian Pacific Railway for the special train. Was it worth it? Indeed it was, for Liffiton, who was averaging a goal a game, paced Montreal to a 4–2 victory.

In March 1902, Charlie was back on a train, this one headed west to Winnipeg. His Montreal club, winners of the league title, had challenged the Winnipeg Vics for the Stanley Cup. It was a best-of-three series played in Winnipeg, with the arena there sold out for each match.

The Vics had captured their title just a few weeks earlier, with a series win over Toronto.

Winnipeg won the opening game by a score of 1–0, but the smaller, faster visitors — nicknamed "the Little Men of Iron" — stormed back to win 5–0 and 2–1 and took the Stanley Cup back east in a hockey bag.

Upon their return to Montreal, the victors were greeted by thousands of admirers who refused to let teams of horses pull their heroes to the team's clubhouse for a party. So, they unhitched the horses and pulled the sleighs themselves, even though the snow was deep and the clubhouse some distance away. There's no doubt Charlie's one-man train ride had been a good deal faster.

GRETZKY BEHIND BARS?

Did you know that Wayne Gretzky once went from the streets of Sault Ste. Marie straight to the slammer? He was thrown in jail when he was just a 17-year-old rookie with the Sault Ste. Marie Greyhounds.

Back then, hazing rookies was a popular part of junior hockey, and as part of his initiation, Wayne was ordered to run down the main street of the city wearing only a jock-strap, with a hockey sock covering his head. As he was jogging along, he was fast on his feet but not as fast as the police car that pulled alongside him, lights flashing.

"What the hell are you doing?" the officer asked.

Wayne tried to explain, and for the first time in his life he used his name to try to get out of this fix. "I'm Wayne Gretzky of the Greyhounds," he told the cop.

"Like hell you are," said the officer. "I know the coach and there's no way he'd associate with weirdos like you. Now get in the back."

Minutes later, Wayne was sitting in a jail cell, worried sick. He was wearing only a jockstrap and thinking, *Boy, this is going to be on the front pages tomorrow and my parents are going to be shocked.*

Just then the door flew open and all his teammates came flooding in, along with the cop who'd hauled him in to the station. They were all laughing hysterically.

"It was all a set-up and I never saw it coming," Wayne said.

WHO KILLED MCCOURT?

The 1906–7 season ended in tragedy with the death of Cornwall star Owen McCourt after an on-ice brawl in a game played on March 6, 1907, against the Ottawa Victorias. McCourt died from a blow to the head from a hockey stick. Criminal charges of manslaughter were filed against Charles Masson of the Vics. The Ottawa player was accused of delivering the fatal blow. But Masson was acquitted when witnesses at his trial stated that one or two other Ottawa hockey players had struck Mr. McCourt in the head before Mr. Masson's blow.

A LEAGUE FOR 30 PLAYERS

When the Pacific Coast Hockey Association (PCHA) was introduced in 1911, there were only three teams competing — Vancouver, Victoria, and New Westminster. Fewer than 30 players, roughly 10 men per team, were required to fill the rosters. On nights when they weren't playing, players often acted as referees and goal judges for the other game going on.

PCHA games were also played on artificial ice — the first league in Canada to do so. The Patrick brothers, Lester and Frank, league organizers, arranged for the construction of two arenas, one in Victoria that seated 4,000 and another in Vancouver, seating 10,500.

The first game of the PCHA was played on January 3, 1912. Cyclone Taylor, the Wayne Gretzky of his day, turned down a contract offer from the Ottawa Hockey Club of the National Hockey Association (NHA) to join the Vancouver team.

After winning five scoring titles in the PCHA, and following his retirement in 1921, Taylor remained involved in hockey. He was named president of the Pacific Coast Hockey League (PCHL) in 1936 and served in that capacity until 1940. He dropped the puck in the ceremonial faceoff that preceded the Vancouver Canucks' first home game when the expansion team joined the NHL in 1970. I had the great pleasure of interviewing him — both of us circling the ice on skates — when he was 90 years old, on an NBC telecast at the old Pacific Coliseum in 1974.

After the 1913–14 regular season, league champion Victoria came east to play the first East-West series for the Stanley Cup against the Toronto Blueshirts. The Blueshirts won, but in the 1914–15 season, Vancouver defeated the Ottawa Senators in a best-of-five series and celebrated as the PCHA's first Stanley Cup champions. The league expanded into the United States in 1914 (Portland, Oregon) and again in 1915 (Seattle, Washington). In 1916, the Portland Rosebuds became the first American team to play for the Stanley Cup. The following year, the Seattle Metropolitans became the first American team to win the Cup.

The PCHA is credited with numerous innovations to the game of hockey, including numbers on jerseys, blue lines and goal creases, forward passing, penalty shots, and playoffs.

ONE TOUGH CUSTOMER

Tie Domi, Tiger Williams, Bob Probert, and Dave Schultz were all NHL tough guys, battlers who will be long remembered for the poundings they laid on their opponents.

Tough guys — less noticeable in today's game — have always been a "drop your gloves, let's go" presence in hockey. And they can be especially mean if their opponents can find a way to get their goat, like teasing them about their name.

Take Winnipeg-born Karl Wilhons Erlendson, who had a name change at an early age and became Carol William Wilson — nickname "Cully." Cully finished his third season of pro hockey in Toronto (1914–15) with 22 goals and 138 penalty minutes in only 20 games. He was a star, and a member of Toronto's first Stanley Cup–winning team.

But opposing players purposely called him Carol. And it made him mad.

"Hey, Carol. How about a date? Wear your best skirt," an opponent might taunt the young player. The gloves would soon come off and the fists would fly.

Cully was born on June 5, 1892, to Sigurdur Erlendson and Metonia Indridadottir, who had immigrated to Manitoba from Iceland. Cully's father, Sigurdur, quickly adopted the English-sounding name Wilson. The *Wilson* fit in, but the newcomers did not. For some reason, Icelanders — and they came to Manitoba in the thousands — were not popular at the time. Eight children grew up with the Wilson name, including one hockey-playing son who heeded one name only: Cully.

By the time he was 17, Cully Wilson was playing senior hockey with the Winnipeg Vikings, a team in an all-Icelandic league. His team was shunned by the snobbish Winnipeg City League. But in 1920, the Winnipeg Falcons, all former Icelanders, won the Allan Cup as the top senior team in Canada and went on to capture the gold medal in the 1920 Olympic Games in Antwerp, Belgium. There's nothing like a gold medal to squash discrimination. Manitobans hailed the Olympic champions. "Who said we never liked the Icelanders? We love 'em now!"

After two seasons in Toronto, Wilson surfaced in Seattle, and he not only took the first penalty in Seattle hockey history but also became the first player to be ejected from a game — in the home opener. That season he accounted for 40 percent of his team's penalties.

During the 1918–19 season, Seattle and Vancouver engaged in several on-ice brawls, with Wilson always in the middle of the melees. One night he clubbed Vancouver's star forward Mickey MacKay with his stick, breaking his jaw and ending his season. Initially, Frank Patrick was furious and suspended Wilson for the rest of the season. But later he bowed to threats by the Seattle players, who vowed not to perform without Wilson, their resident tough guy.

What could Patrick do? He was running a three-team league, and the loss of one club would be disastrous. He finally caved in and fined Wilson a measly $50.

During the now-famous 1919 Stanley Cup Final between Seattle and the visiting Montreal Canadiens, Wilson scored what might have been the Stanley Cup–winning goal in Game 4. It came at the end of the first period, and Seattle fans triggered an explosive celebration that turned to fury when the goal was waved off. It was judged that time had ended before the puck crossed the line.

The game continued, went into overtime, then was declared a draw. Too bad it wasn't played to a finish, for a major epidemic was about to leave a devastating mark on the teams and the competition.

The Habs won the next game to tie the series, but players on both teams looked sluggish on the ice, and many were feverish. One reporter described Cully's performance thusly: "Wilson, who had a body built of scrap iron and a never-give-up spirit, limped to the bench and hung helpless over the railing. He was carried to the locker room, incoherently protesting that he was able to continue. Manager Pete Muldoon looked for a replacement, but there was no one. The bench was empty."

Game 6, scheduled for two days later, was never played. The horrific flu outbreak that swept across North America that spring, resulting in thousands of deaths, forced the cancellation of the series. Several players became gravely ill. Montreal's Bad Joe Hall, a tough customer like Wilson, was rushed to hospital, where he died a few days later.

For the first time in Stanley Cup history, the season ended without a champion. By a split second, Wilson missed becoming a three-time Stanley Cup winner.

In the off-season, President Patrick decided that Wilson should be punished for his unruly behaviour that year and suspended him for the entire 1919–20 season. Wilson shrugged, thumbed his nose at Patrick, and left Seattle, seeking greener pastures. He wound up back in Toronto — with the St. Pats in the NHL — and went on to lead his new league in penalties.

Cully Wilson died in Seattle in 1962.

ONE BIZARRE GOAL

Here's a tale of one of hockey's strangest goals, scored by former NHL all-star Jack Adams of the famed Vancouver Millionaires — a goal he should never have been given credit for. In the final game of the 1920–21 season, Vancouver beat Victoria 11–8. During that high-scoring affair, Adams accidentally scored — on his own goaltender! The reason the goal was so bizarre is that the official scorer credited it to Adams, and it was added to his total in the individual scoring race. Have you ever heard of such a thing? Why he got credit for the goal has never been made clear. But he did; in fact, the strange goal vaulted him into fifth place in the individual scoring race.

Adams would later become more famous as a coach and manager than he was as a player. During his 36 years with the Detroit Red Wings, as coach and general manager, he became the second winningest coach in Wings' history, behind Mike Babcock. Adams is the only hockey man to win the Stanley Cup as a player, coach, and manager.

SCORERS SIZZLE IN NHL'S FIRST SEASON

In 1917, the NHL was organized during a meeting in Montreal. Initially, four teams comprised the new NHL: the Toronto Hockey Club, Montreal Canadiens, Montreal Wanderers, and Ottawa Senators. Toronto — a team without an official nickname, though they were known as the Blueshirts — almost didn't gain admission to the new league. A franchise was granted to Toronto only after a Quebec City club dropped out.

On the eve of the NHL opener, two of the clubs were threatened by a concerned arena owner in Montreal. He told both clubs using his rink — the Canadiens and the Wanderers — that he was disgusted with the poor calibre of hockey they'd displayed in the past and warned them he would turf them both from his building if they didn't improve. "I'll reserve the ice time for pleasure skating," he threatened, "if you fellows don't shape up."

The Wanderers won their opening game 10–9 over Toronto before a slim crowd of just 700 spectators (soldiers in uniform were allowed in free). On the eve of the Wanderers' sixth game, their home rink, the Westmount Arena, burned down. The club was invited to play in Hamilton but declined. The Canadiens, who also played home games at the Westmount Rink, relocated to the tiny 3,200-seat Jubilee Arena. Once the greatest team in hockey, the Wanderers dropped out of the new league, never to return. Their NHL record shows one victory and five defeats in six games played; they allowed 35 goals, almost six per game. A few seasons earlier, they had won 10, lost none, and scored 105 goals, more than 10 per game.

The best player on ice during that first NHL season was Joe Malone, acquired by Montreal from Quebec, who scored 44 goals in 20 games — a record that has never been broken. The Canadiens won their opener over Ottawa 7–4, with Malone scoring five goals for the Habs.

Some odd things happened in the league's first season. When the Ottawa Senators skated out for a game in Toronto in January, the Senators bench was empty — they had no substitutes on hand. Toronto reciprocated by emptying its own bench. It was the only NHL game ever played with the minimum of 12 players involved.

In another game, police arrested Bad Joe Hall of Montreal and Alf Skinner of Toronto after they tried to decapitate each other in a vicious stick-swinging duel. Both were hauled into court, where a judge — obviously a fan — released them with suspended sentences.

During the season, Ken Randall of Toronto owed the NHL $35 in fines. "Pay up before the next game or you won't play," he was told. Randall produced $32 in bills and 300 pennies. When a league official refused to accept the pennies, Randall placed them in a neat pile on the ice. A teammate skated by and whacked the pile with his stick, scattering pennies in all directions. The Toronto players were forced to scoop them up while Randall borrowed suitable folding money to pay the rest of his fine.

Three players that first season who scored 20 or more goals set goals-per-game averages that have never been topped. Montreal's Joe Malone, with his 44 goals in 20 games, averaged 2.20 goals per game. Cy Denneny (Ottawa), with 36 goals in 20 games, finished in second place with a 1.80 average. Newsy Lalonde (Montreal) scored 23 goals in 14 games, an average of 1.64. No modern-day player has come close to those averages.

Toronto met Vancouver to contend for the Stanley Cup that season, with Toronto winning the deciding game 2–1 and Corb Denneny scoring the winning goal. Once a lacrosse prodigy, Denneny signed a pro lacrosse contract when he was just 14. He was also a sprinter and tied the 100-yard world record in a meet in Toronto. Corb and his brother, Cy, each scored six goals in a game two months apart, in January and March of 1921, respectively — both in games against Hamilton. But on January 31, 1920, in the previous season, Joe Malone of the Quebec Bulldogs scored seven goals in a 10–6 victory over Toronto. It's an NHL record that's stood for 100 years. Malone pumped in 146 career goals in 125 games, a pace that modern-day scoring wizards have never been able to match.

An added scoring fact: Only two modern-day players have scored six goals in a game — Leafs captain Darryl Sittler and the Blues' Red Berenson. (Berenson is the only player to score six times in a road game.)

MY FAVOURITE STICK

Hall of Famer Reg Noble's hockey career began in 1916–17 and ended in 1933–34. But it's his famous stick I want to tell you about.

When Noble was traded to the Montreal Maroons, he had already used his stick for two seasons in Toronto. It must have been made of ironwood. Noble used it in another 100 games in Montreal before being traded to Detroit, where he used it for another season. Then he autographed the stick and presented it to the manager of the Detroit Olympia Stadium, who nailed it to the wall of his office. Later, Noble came out of retirement to play with Detroit. He broke into the manager's office, pried his favourite stick off the wall, and used it for yet another season.

THE CUP HEADS SOUTH

With Seattle the newest member of the NHL, it may come as a surprise to learn that Seattle was the first U.S. city to capture the Stanley Cup. In 1917, playing on home ice, the Seattle Metropolitans beat the Montreal Canadiens by four games to one in the final series. In Game 2, fans were shocked when Montreal star Newsy Lalonde turned on the referee and speared him in the groin. Lalonde was fined $25 and expelled from the match. The referee had to be carried off the ice. Leading 9–1 in the final game, Seattle fans became "a wild, howling mass of humanity," according to a local newspaper. "They stood and cheered until the iron girders of the arena roof rattled."

PUNCH PUTS THE PUCK IN

During the 1921–22 season, Ottawa's Punch Broadbent potted goals in 16 consecutive games, establishing a record that has never been broken. The previous record holder was Joe Malone, with goals in 14 straight games. Another amazing feat that season was Ottawa's Frank Nighbor's ability to play six consecutive games at centre ice without requiring a rest. What's more, he averaged a goal per game!

HELLO, CANADA!

On March 22, 1923, Toronto games were broadcast on radio for the first time. Play-by-play broadcaster Foster Hewitt worked from a small glassed-in booth rinkside at the Mutual Street Arena in Toronto. Foster would soon become as famous across Canada as any of the NHL players. He would end his career in 1972, calling the gripping eight-game series between the Soviets and Team Canada, won by Team Canada on Paul Henderson's dramatic last-minute goal.

There are three Hewitts in the Hockey Hall of Fame: Foster's dad, W.A. Hewitt; Foster himself; and his son, Bill.

CLANCY DID IT ALL

Imagine an NHL star playing every position, including goal, in a Stanley Cup playoff game. In 1923, Ottawa's Frank "King" Clancy's versatility created the oddball situation. Clancy's team, the Ottawa Senators, met two western teams in back-to-back Stanley Cup championships, with both series being played in Vancouver.

After the Senators eliminated the Vancouver club, the PCHL champs, they were challenged by a team from Edmonton, the Western Canada Hockey League (WCHL) titlists, in a second series for Lord Stanley's famous mug. The Senators were riddled with injuries, and 19-year-old Clancy, in the second game, was called on to play both defensive positions and all three forward positions. Then Clint Benedict, Ottawa's goaltender, was penalized. In those days, goalies served their own time in the box. Benedict gave his goal stick to Clancy and said, "Kid, you take over. I'll be right back." Clancy shrugged and took his place between the pipes. He was not scored upon, the Senators won the series, and the teenage Clancy skated off the ice, unaware he'd just made a bit of hockey history. That was the way Clancy described his feat to me when we collaborated on his memoir back in 1968. But recently, one historian claims that Clancy had played every position but goal in a game in the previous series against Vancouver. But whether in a game or a series, he's the only player to do so.

Clancy also helped make history in Ottawa one night when he was a young member of the Senators. A cold front had swept over Ottawa and temperatures plunged to minus 30 degrees. Clancy, along with teammates Morley Bruce and Frank Boucher, were the subs on the Ottawa bench. But most players were 60-minute men in those days, so the three subs ran for the dressing room, where they huddled around the pot-bellied stove. If the coach needed one of them, he'd ring a bell from the bench — one bell for Clancy, two bells for Bruce, and three bells for Boucher. The three subs got warm and loosened their laces. Then the bell rang. Three bells. But Boucher broke a lace, so Clancy dashed out. "I want Boucher, not you," the coach barked. So Clancy retreated. But still no Boucher. The crowd began to jeer, and the referee began to fume, threatening a delay-of-game penalty.

Things calmed down when Boucher appeared, but the league stepped in the following day with a new rule: All players must be on the bench during a game.

Later, during his long career in the sport, Clancy became a coach, a manager, and a referee. And a Hall of Famer, as well!

STRIKE ONE

In 1924–25, the NHL added six games to the regular season, and the extra workload led to a player revolt in Hamilton, Ontario.

Hamilton? In the NHL?

Indeed it was. In fact, the Hamilton Tigers had risen from last place to first place, and the Stanley Cup was only a couple of playoff victories away.

But first, there was a little matter of compensation for the six extra games the Tigers had played. Shorty Green, captain of the Tigers, had learned that other club owners had shelled out for the extra workload. Surely the Tigers would follow suit, and Shorty figured that $200 per man was a fair amount.

"There'll be no extra pay," roared owner Percy Thompson. NHL president Frank Calder backed him up.

"Then we'll go on strike," the players threatened. "To hell with the playoffs and the Stanley Cup."

Calder immediately suspended the Tigers, fined each man $200, and decided that the winner of a semi-final series between Montreal and Toronto would compete in that spring's playoffs. Montreal advanced while the Hamilton rebels fumed.

Before the next season rolled around, New York investors had purchased the Hamilton franchise for $75,000 and shifted it to Madison Square Garden, where the team surfaced under a new name — the New York Americans. And the Hamilton players, before being reinstated, were ordered to apologize in writing to President Calder for their mercenary attitude. As for the rebellious Shorty Green, his induction into the Hockey Hall of Fame in 1962 came as a surprise. He played in a mere 103 NHL games over four seasons and scored a modest 33 goals and 53 points. Those don't sound like Hall of Fame numbers to me.

PICK YOUR WINNER, MY LADY

In 1925, Lady Byng, the wife of Governor General Lord Byng, donated a trophy in her name to the NHL player who best exhibited sportsmanlike conduct and a high level of ability. Lady Byng was allowed to name the winner, and she selected Frank Nighbor of Ottawa, one of her favourite players, as the first recipient. Late in the 1925 season, Nighbor was invited to Rideau Hall after a game. Lady Byng showed him a gleaming new trophy and asked him if he thought it an appropriate award for the NHL's most gentlemanly player. Nighbor said it would be a grand gift to hockey, and to his surprise, Lady Byng presented him with the trophy on the spot, making him the first recipient of the Lady Byng Trophy. A year earlier, he'd been named the first winner of the Hart Trophy as the league's most valuable player (MVP).

I've always suspected that Lady Byng had a secret crush on Frank Nighbor, the man known as "the Pembroke Peach."

HO HUM, JUST ANOTHER GOOSE EGG

On February 18, 1928, goalie Alec Connell of the Ottawa Senators recorded his sixth consecutive shutout with a 1–0 win over Montreal. Connell's mark has never been surpassed. The goaltender recorded 15 shutouts that season but was upstaged by little George Hainsworth of the Canadiens, who blanked opposing teams 22 times over 44 games. Why so many shutouts? Forward passing was not allowed in those days.

In the 2003–4 season, a modern-day goaltender managed to post a shutout in five consecutive games. Journeyman keeper Brian Boucher of the Phoenix Coyotes shut out the Kings, Stars, Hurricanes, Capitals, and Wild — a streak that ended on January 11, 2004, against Atlanta. Boucher came close to making it six in a row, but Atlanta's Randy Robitaille scored a fluke goal on him early in the first period — the Thrashers' only goal of the game. For a span of two weeks,

BRIAN MCFARLANE

Boucher was the greatest goaltender in hockey, and besting his five straight goose eggs will be a challenge.

As for career shutouts, Martin Brodeur's mark of 125 may be even more of a challenge. Roberto Luongo retired in 2019 with 77, the highest among active goalies.

Here is a list of NHL goalies with 80 or more career shutouts:

Marty Brodeur 125
Terry Sawchuk 103
George Hainsworth 94
Glenn Hall 84
Jacques Plante 82
Dominik Hasek 81
Tiny Thompson 81
Alec Connell 81

THE TEAM THAT COULDN'T SCORE

During the 1928–29 season, the Chicago Blackhawks set records for futility that have lasted for almost 90 years. In just their third NHL season, the Blackhawks won a measly seven games over the 44-game schedule. During one eight-game stretch, they were shut out eight straight times. Over the course of the season, the Hawks were blanked a total of 21 times, or in almost 50 percent of their games!

And their so-called scorers were pathetic, managing only 33 goals all season, fewer than one per game. Forward Vic Ripley led the Hawks scorers with 11 goals and two assists for 13 points, an embarrassing total. The Hawks' second leading scorer was Johnny Gottselig, who tallied five goals and three assists for eight points. Fortunately, in 1928–29, the Hawks had Charlie Gardiner in goal or they might not have won a single game. Gardiner finished among the league's best net-minders, posting five shutouts and a 1.93 goals-against average in 44 games.

In 1934, Gardiner led his team to the Stanley Cup, losing only one of eight playoff games. He was treated to a bumpy ride through Chicago's Loop in a wheelbarrow — winner of an unusual bet. But his greatest performance turned out to be his last. Two months later, Gardiner died suddenly of a brain hemorrhage in Winnipeg. He was only 29 years old.

FIRST GAME A DAZZLING SUCCESS

the New York Rangers made their Madison Square Garden debut against the talented Montreal Maroons, the defending Stanley Cup champions. A near-unanimous choice by most to finish last in the American Division of the 10-team NHL, the Rangers had been a sorry-looking club during training camp, and manager Conn Smythe, a newcomer to professional hockey, bore the brunt of the blame. But the critics were wrong. Smythe had assembled a top-flight club that included the Cook brothers, Bill and Bun, and Frank Boucher, all stars of the defunct Western Hockey League. Ivan "Ching" Johnson and Clarence "Taffy" Abel were balding belters who could heave opponents over the boards or lay them flat out on the ice. He added goaltender Lorne Chabot and ironman Murray

Murdoch, who played the next 11 seasons without missing a game. But Rangers president John Hammond fired Smythe during training camp and replaced him with Lester Patrick, a more experienced coach and manager. The articulate Patrick, then 42, would guide the Rangers from behind the bench for the next 13 years.

For the opener, most of the male fans were attired in tuxedos, while the ladies wore fashionable evening gowns.

Rangers star Frank Boucher would later recall that the opening game was as "rough as any I ever played. The grunts from players slammed into the ice or boards could be heard 20 rows up."

Only one goal was scored, and it came when the Cooks teamed up to beat Maroons goalie Clint Benedict, who, years later, would introduce the first face mask to the NHL.

The Rangers received a prolonged ovation at the game's finish.

"Did you hear them cheer?" a player shrieked. "They love us here."

Lester Patrick shook hands all around. "Boys, this franchise will be a huge success. This is just the beginning."

SHRIMP GETS IN THE GAME. OR DOES HE?

In the '30s, the Toronto Maple Leafs, with several players sidelined by injury, limped into the NHL playoffs one year. Desperate for help, the team called on a local lad, Shrimp McPherson, to don the blue and white. In the event of another injury, Shrimp would get his big-league chance.

Midway through the playoff game, Shrimp's moment came. He was instructed to replace an injured Leaf who was hobbling from the ice to the bench. In his eagerness to play, Shrimp jumped onto the ice too soon. His skates had no sooner hit the Gardens' slick surface than the referee signalled a penalty. "Too many men on the ice!" he roared, pointing at Shrimp.

Red-faced, McPherson headed back to the bench while one of his teammates was sent to the penalty box. He didn't get another chance.

According to hockey historian Mike Ferriman, Shrimp has the dubious distinction of being the only player in NHL history to incur a penalty without ever playing a single second in the NHL.

NHL records show no evidence that Shrimp played in that NHL game or any other. But he enjoyed a fine minor-league career and was living in St. Louis when the Blues gained entry to an expanded NHL in 1967. It was there he finally made his way back to the NHL — as assistant trainer with the Blues. He passed away in Oakland, California, in 1974, following a game between the Blues and California Golden Seals.

McPherson's obituary began: "Former Toronto Maple Leaf centre [but was he?] and assistant trainer for the St. Louis Blues …"

Special thanks to Maple Leafs team historian Mike Ferriman for sharing the tale of Alex "Shrimp" McPherson.

ICING AND MORE ICING

The Boston Bruins and the New York Americans played a pair of unique games during the 1931–32 season. On December 8, 1931, in Boston, the Americans shot the puck down the ice at every opportunity. Although boring to the fans, it was a great way to take the pressure off while playing a superior team. Since no rules had yet been devised to prevent "icing the puck," the Bruins spent most of the evening chasing the disc back into their own zone. That night it happened 61 times, leaving the Boston players angry and frustrated.

Bruins owner Charles Adams vowed to get even. On January 3, 1932, in a game played on New York ice, the Bruins "iced the puck" 87 times. The two games rank as perhaps the most boring ever played. NHL president Frank Calder soon introduced a rule designed to curb icing the puck.

SHOOT FROM THE CIRCLE

The penalty shot was not invented in the NHL but in the Pacific Coast Hockey Association. It was introduced during the 1921–22 season by the Patrick brothers, Lester and Frank, who had created the league. The first free shot was taken on December 6, 1921, and the first goal was scored six days later by Tom Dunderdale, an Australian who played with Victoria. The shot was taken from one of three dots painted on the ice 35 feet from the goal. Players had to skate to the dot and shoot the puck from there. In 1974, Dunderdale became the only Aussie to be inducted into the Hockey Hall of Fame.

The penalty shot was introduced in the NHL for the 1934–35 season. Initially, the puck was placed in a 10-foot circle, 38 feet out from the goal. The player could shoot while standing in the circle, or he could shoot while moving into the circle. The goaltender had to remain stationary, standing no more than a foot in front of his net until the puck was shot. The Canadiens' Armand Mondou took the first NHL penalty shot on November 10, 1934, but was thwarted by Leafs goalie George Hainsworth. Three days later, Ralph "Scotty" Bowman of the St. Louis Eagles (St. Louis was in the league back then) scored the first penalty-shot goal in NHL history.

The strangest penalty-shot I ever saw was one taken at the Montreal Forum by Montreal's Bobby Rousseau in the 1961–62 season. Rousseau shot at Boston goalie Ed Johnston from just inside the blue line — and scored!

The strangest penalty shot story I ever heard came from the lips of my old-timer teammate for many seasons — former NHLer Jackie Hamilton: "I was awarded a penalty shot in the early '40s," he recalled, "when there were two types of penalty shots — a major and a minor one. So I stood in the circle and fired one in the net. But the other team complained, telling the ref I should have been given a major penalty shot, which meant I could skate in from centre ice. The ref asked me to help him out by shooting again. I said 'Sure' and skated in from centre and scored on a second shot. I'm the only player in history to score two penalty-shot goals on one penalty-shot call!"

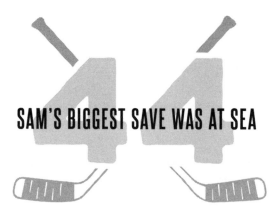

SAM'S BIGGEST SAVE WAS AT SEA

If Chicago Blackhawks goalie Sam LoPresti is remembered at all, it's for a game he played against Boston on March 4, 1941. He was credited with 80 saves on 83 shots in a 3–2 loss to the visitors. The 80 saves he made that night remain an NHL record.

LoPresti joined the U.S. Navy during the Second World War, and in February 1943 was aboard a merchant ship in the South Atlantic when a German U-boat blew the vessel apart with torpedoes. LoPresti and 29 shipmates scrambled aboard a single lifeboat, which drifted on the ocean for more than a month. Survivors shared strictly rationed food and water (until a steady downpour replenished the water supply). LoPresti won praise from his shipmates after he killed a dolphin with a knife, providing life-saving food during their ordeal.

On the 42nd day, LoPresti, who was on watch, finally spotted land. It was the coast of Brazil. The survivors were picked up by a Brazilian ship and taken to hospital. LoPresti had lost 74 pounds during his ordeal. The Navy had reported him missing in action and his family had given him up for dead.

"Facing 83 shots in a hockey game is child's play compared to facing those torpedoes from a U-boat," he later told a reporter.

MOSEY WAS MIGHTY FAST

On March 23, 1952, the Chicago Blackhawks journeyed to New York to close out their dismal regular season against the Rangers. The Hawks had won only 16 games and were destined for another last-place finish — their third in a row. Earlier in the season, Chicago winger Bill Mosienko had mentioned to a team-mate, "Looks like I'll never get to play on a Stanley Cup winner, but I'd sure like to do something that I'll be remembered for."

In the final game of that season, Mosienko got his wish. Fewer than 2,500 fans witnessed the feat. A few years ago, in Winnipeg, he recalled his shining moment: "I scored three goals on a rookie goalie named Anderson in record time — 21 seconds. Gus Bodnar was my centre and he set a rec-ord, too — for the three fastest assists. We won the game 7–6 after trailing 6–2. Poor Anderson never played another game. And that's the mark I was destined to leave."

"WATCH OUT, REF! HERE IT COMES!"

During the 1952 playoffs, Pete and Jerry Cusimano, sons of a Detroit fishmonger, took a dead octopus to the Olympia for what turned out to be the final game between the Red Wings and the Canadiens for the Stanley Cup. Because the Wings had already won seven consecutive playoff games — four over Toronto and three more over Montreal — the nutty Cusimano brothers reasoned that the eight tentacles of a stinking octopus thrown on the ice would bring the Wings a final bit of good luck. The splat of their octopus hitting the ice did the trick. The Red Wings shut out Montreal 3–0 that night, and the Cusimanos enjoyed some backslapping from their friends at the fish market the next day.

Octopus-tossing then became an annual rite of spring in Detroit. "Those Cusimano brothers always made the officials a little uneasy," said former NHL ref Red Storey. "We'd wonder when those little buggers were going to throw that ugly thing. We were on octopus watch."

TWO OBSCURE RECORDS

Jerry Toppazzini was a colourful player for the Boston Bruins many years ago, and he was always an easy interview. I asked him once about two records he held.

"Well, I'm proud to say I hold the NHL record for scoring four goals in a game. I scored two on the Montreal goalie and then — accidentally, of course — I scored two on the Boston goalie. Somehow, that feat never made it to the NHL record book.

"Before that — this would be in my second or third game in the NHL, and we were playing in Chicago — Sugar Jim Henry, our goalie, took a shot in the nose and both his eyes closed tight. There were about nine minutes to play and our coach, Lynn Patrick, said, 'Toppazzini, you play in goal.'

"So I finished the game and didn't give up a goal. Stopped some pretty good shots, too. I actually played in three different games in goal. No backup goalies then and I was the last regular player to be one. Must have played 15, 16 minutes in all. That's another record they didn't put in the book. You better put it in one of yours.

"Put this fact in, too. After a game, a father approached me and asked me to sign his son's program. While I'm signing, the kid looks up at me and says, 'How old are you, Mr. Toppazzini?' Well, I was 35 years old, but I said to the kid, 'Son, how old do you think I am?' He stared up at me and said, 'Maybe 45?'

"I said, 'Son, you're out by 10 years.'

"And he said, 'You mean you're *55*?'"

A NIGHT FOR MARCEL

In 1963, the many friends of Red Wings defenceman Marcel Pronovost organized a special "night" for him. But his night didn't take place at the Detroit Olympia. It was held at the Forum — in Montreal.

The citizens of Beauharnois, Quebec, Pronovost's hometown, were not wealthy. They couldn't afford to travel to Detroit for the ceremony, so they asked Frank Selke, the general manager of the Montreal Canadiens, if they could honour Marcel during a Wings-Canadiens game at the Forum. Such a thing had never been done before, but Selke gave his approval.

Tradition dictates that a new car be presented to the guest of honour on such an occasion, and the citizens of Beauharnois were proud to present Marcel with the keys to a gleaming new car — the latest model — at centre ice.

But Marcel's friends had managed to raise only half the price of the car. They took Marcel aside and explained the situation. "Perhaps you could help by paying for the other half," it was suggested. Marcel was surprised, of course. But the folks back home had been his greatest supporters.

"Sure," he said. "I'll buy half the car."

Marcel Pronovost is the only NHL player honoured with a night in an opposing team's city, and the only one who paid for half of the new car he received!

HALL'S FANTASTIC STREAK

In modern-day hockey, it's not unusual for an NHL team to employ two, three, even half a dozen goaltenders over the course of a gruelling NHL season. But until the mid-1960s, teams relied solely on one man to play between the pipes. And no team relied more heavily on its goaltender than the Chicago Blackhawks, who were blessed with the best — Glenn Hall.

Hall was a durable superstar who was always ready and willing to play. He may not have looked willing, though, because he threw up before almost every game.

"Really, Glenn?" rookie Dennis Hull asked. "Do you always have to throw up?"

"No, just since you joined the club," was the goalie's reply.

Over many seasons, the games piled up and the records began to fall: 300 consecutive games, then 400, then 500. And don't forget, Hall played without a mask, risking cuts and concussions with every start.

On the night of November 7, 1962, Chicago played host to the Boston Bruins. On this night, Hall scrapped his customary routine — an energetic wrestling match with the team trainer to settle pre-game jitters. He couldn't wrestle because he was suffering from excruciating back pain. But when the Hawks took the ice that night, Hall was standing calmly in his crease.

In the opening minutes of play, Boston's Murray Oliver fired a shot at Hall and the puck flew right between his legs. He simply couldn't move fast enough to stop it. He skated slowly to the Chicago bench and headed for the dressing room. His departure, in his 503rd consecutive game, brought to an end a string of more than 33,000 uninterrupted minutes of goaltending. Hall's incredible ironman streak was over.

It's safe to say that's one record that will never be broken.

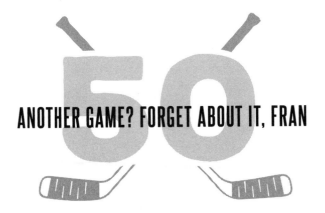

ANOTHER GAME? FORGET ABOUT IT, FRAN

Women have been eager participants in hockey almost from the beginning. From the beginning of the last century, male players recruited sisters, mothers, wives and girlfriends to join them on frozen ponds for long games of shinny on ice. In time, women formed teams with creative names: the Snowflakes, the Floradoras, the Mighty Maidens, and even the Old Hens. One of the pioneers — a goalie — told me how she secretly kept her goals against average down. "It was the long skirt era and I wore a skirt extra long. And I put buckshot in the hem of the skirt. When I bent over in goal I'd spread my skirt out. That hem stopped a lot of pucks." With women's hockey growing more popular every year, the future is bright for the girls in the game. But it hasn't always been rosy.

I once chatted with Fran Westman, a University of Toronto hockey player in the early 1930s, who was one of the stars of a team called the Vagabonds. For a game in Port Dover in 1933, posters advertised Miss Westman as the most "outstanding lady hockeyist in Ontario." But did she excel in the contest? No. Newly married, Fran's husband refused to let her play: "She had another game to play two days later," he explained, "and two games in one week is too much for a woman — in my opinion."

His bride was left fuming. But she bowed to her husband's wishes. "Today, I'd just grab my skates and go play," she told me. "I'm still upset there were posters announcing my appearance and I didn't show up."

THE RIGHT TO PLAY

Justine Blainey-Broker, a player of note when she was a young girl in Toronto, told me a gripping story of her attempt to break the gender barrier in hockey. In the mid-1980s, when she was 12 years old, she sought a position on a team — a boys' team.

She knew she was just as skilled as the boys, so she thought, *why not play on a boys' team?* But the Metro Toronto Hockey League (MTHL) stopped her in her skates. She wasn't allowed to play with boys, and the Ontario Hockey Association backed the Metro League. No girls allowed.

Frustrated, Justine said she was determined to fight for her rights, and when lawyer Anna Fraser heard of her plight, she offered to help — pro bono.

Justine never anticipated the cruel treatment she'd receive from those who thought she was trying to play where she didn't belong.

It was shocking. Picture a young girl with a hockey bag and a zest for the game entering an arena and being spat on and doused with coffee. Her mother — a single parent — was unable to defend her daughter when she was shunned and cursed. On one occasion, little Justine was pushed down the stairs in a Toronto subway station.

I wrote about her battle back then in my book *Proud Past, Bright Future: One Hundred Years of Canadian Women's Hockey*, but I had no idea at the time that she'd been the recipient of such ugly, inexcusable treatment.

Now 44 years old and a practising chiropractor, Justine looks back on those days with some regret. "It was hurtful for me, but hopefully it was helpful for women's hockey," she says. "In girls' hockey, I was hated. I was told I was a lesbian. I was told I'd never have kids. That no man would ever marry me. When you're 14 or 15, that really hurts."

The case dragged on because of a lot of legal wrangling. Finally, in 1987, the issue went before an Ontario Human Rights Commission board of inquiry. Ian Springate was the commissioner.

That inquiry heard so-called experts say that girls playing on a boys' team distorts a young woman's personality, and that girls were physically "out of their league" when they tried to compete with boys.

While waiting for a decision, Justine played on girls' teams and practised with boys' teams. Finally, in December,

1987, Springate ruled in Justine's favour. Discrimination on the basis of sex in athletic activities became unlawful in Ontario.

Justine was pleased — but at age 15 and at five foot four, she wasn't sure she was eager to play with or against the huskier teenage boys. John Gardiner, president of the MTHL, was unhappy with the ruling. "That inquiry cost us well over $100,000," he growled. Fran Rider, president of the Ontario Women's Hockey Association, thought the ruling was a "negative step" for women in hockey and that "the best girls should stay together and develop the game. We weren't against Justine but against the principle. She is a good person."

At the age of 19, after three seasons in boys' hockey, Justine joined the University of Toronto Lady Blues, where she spearheaded a campaign to save the women's hockey program at the school. Later, she played with Brampton of the National Women's Hockey League.

Some hurt and fear remain, she says, and it is rare for Justine to ride a bus or subway alone. But she still plays recreational hockey twice a week.

THESE WOMEN CAN REALLY PLAY

The 1990s brought some welcome surprises to women's hockey: record registration of female players, women joining men's professional ranks (three female goalies won games while performing on men's pro teams in the minor leagues; one of them, Manon Rheaume, was given a tryout by the Tampa Bay Lightning and played in an NHL pre-season game). Bona fide world championships were held in Ottawa in 1990, in Finland in 1992, in Lake Placid in 1994, and in Kitchener, Ontario, in 1997. Canadian teams went undefeated in those tournaments, compiling a 20–0 record in international competition.

Then came the 1998 Winter Olympics in Nagano, Japan, with women's hockey occupying a global stage. Team USA upset Canada to win the first ever Olympic gold medal.

Four years later in Salt Lake City, Canada sought revenge. After compiling an impressive 31-0-0 record in pre-Olympic play, the Canadian women dethroned the defending champions with a 3–2 score. Team Canada had to deal with 11 U.S. power plays en route to their stunning triumph.

In 2018, at the Pyeongchang Olympics, the United States won gold again after a 20-year wait, edging Canada 3–2 in the gold medal game.

Kendall Coyne Schofield, a 26-year-old star on the U.S. team, became the first woman to compete at the NHL's 2018 All-Star Game. She amazed everyone with a time of 14.346 seconds in the speed skating event, finishing one second behind winner Connor McDavid.

DECADES OF CHANGE

In 2019, more than 200 of the world's most talented players decided they would no longer compete in North America until a single professional league was established. Their decision came after a Canadian pro league ceased operations and a five-team U.S. league was deemed unsuitable. The NHL, with several member teams supporting pro clubs for women, approves of the one-league concept.

Financial guru Terrence Corcoran offers this proposal. "The National Hockey League Players' Association could, as an organization, join the NHL owners in a voluntary allocation of a small part of the NHL players' salaries (which, remember, average $3 million a year) to raise incomes in the women's league. Would a 10 percent hockey-equity tax be too much? How about 5 percent? The 31 teams in the NHL each have team salary caps of $83 million, which means that a 5 percent equity tax would raise roughly $4 million from every NHL team, for a league total of about $125 million."

A novel idea. Probably won't happen.

Retired Canadian superstar Hayley Wickenheiser says, "I would have loved to be around to play true professional women's hockey, where you're really paid and it's really legitimate. That's the one thing I wish had happened in my playing days. The reality is it's going to happen when the NHL decides it's going to happen. That's the true answer. I don't know when that is, but I know it's going to happen."

FRANCIS FIGHTS THREE FIREMEN

Goal judges are no longer part of hockey, gone like the rover and the wooden sticks. In hockey's formative years, goal judges stood out on the ice, behind each net, and they waved a hankie when the puck went in. Today, goal judges have been replaced in the NHL by cameras and video reviews.

Arthur Reichert was a goal judge at the old and new Madison Square Garden in New York. Over his 60-year career, Reichert signalled about 12,000 goals. But one he signalled on the night of November 22, 1964, caused Rangers coach and manager Emile Francis to go ballistic.

One day, Francis told me the story:

"We're leading Gordie Howe and the Red Wings 2–1 with time running out when Norm Ullman of the Wings takes a quick shot and play carries on. Then the ref suddenly blows his whistle and talks to Reichert, the goal judge. Then he gives Detroit a goal. What the hell! I'm so mad I take off around the rink and I get to the goal judge, who was sitting on a stool, and I start giving him a blast. But there were three firemen close by, drinking beer and yelling at me to screw off. So when one of them made a move toward me, I nailed him with a punch and knocked him right over the seats. That triggered a brawl, and all the Rangers on the ice see this and they race down … to help me. Right up over the high glass they go — one, two, three.

"After a long skirmish, my new suit was in shreds and I had cuts under both eyes.

"The next day, I was told the firemen were suing me for a million dollars!

"Well, it took seven years before the case went to court in Brooklyn, and when the jury walked in right in front of me, one juror put his hand out and said, 'Good luck, Coach.'

"'Mistrial!' the judge shouted.

"Yeah, the judge declared a mistrial. But we were back two years later, and this time there was a different judge and jury and the firemen were awarded $100,000.

"And get this. One of them asked me for my autograph when the trial was over.

"So I'm the guy who caused the league to put the goal judge in a booth from then on so nobody could get to him."

FANS ASSAULT LEAGUE PRESIDENT, THEN RIOT

On St. Patrick's Day 1955, the Canadiens hosted the Red Wings at the Montreal Forum. But the contest lasted only half a period.

Montreal fans were livid over the suspension of their hero, Rocket Richard, who, in a previous game, had clubbed the Bruins' Hal Laycoe over the head with his stick. League president Clarence Campbell suspended the Habs star for the rest of the season and the playoffs. At the time, Richard was all but assured of winning the scoring title — his first.

Richard fans gathered outside the Forum on the afternoon of the game. Some carried banners reading "We want Campbell."

Campbell arrived late for the game and was promptly pelted with eggs and tomatoes. One young hoodlum approached the league president in a friendly way, offering his hand, and then punched him in the face. Inside, when a tear gas bomb landed on the ice, the players were ordered back to their dressing rooms. The fire director instructed the building to be cleared.

While panic was narrowly averted inside the building, the mob outside became uncontrollable. Screams and shouts filled the air, and rocks were thrown at the building. Windows were smashed. The mob swept down Ste. Catherine Street, damaging cars, starting fires, and looting stores.

Campbell was lucky to escape without serious injury. But he would not rescind the suspension of Richard, who lost the scoring title to his teammate, Bernie "Boom Boom" Geoffrion.

Many Montrealers are convinced the Habs lost the Stanley Cup that year to Detroit because of Richard's suspension. After that season, the Habs went on to win five Cups in a row, still a record. But it might easily have been six.

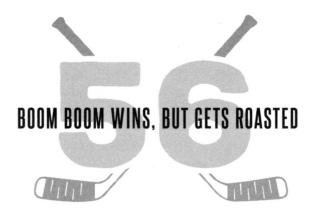

BOOM BOOM WINS, BUT GETS ROASTED

Bernie "Boom Boom" Geoffrion found no joy or satisfaction in winning the individual scoring championship in 1955. In fact, it caused him more suffering than he ever anticipated.

"When I tied the Rocket for the NHL scoring lead in 1955, and then finished ahead of him because of his suspension, the Montreal fans went wild. At the Forum, they booed the hell out of me. Yeah, they wanted to kill me — really kill me. For days, my wife, even though she was the daughter of Howie Morenz, was hysterical; she was getting these calls — angry people who said they were going to blow up my house with my kids inside. A crowd gathered outside and there was talk of lynching me. The cops came and surrounded my home. I hired some private detectives for protection. All because I had more points than the Rocket. And because his suspension cost him his only chance to win the scoring title. People loved the Rocket. It was obvious they didn't like me. What did they expect me to do in those final few games — shoot wide of the net, make bad passes? Sit out those games?"

In the long history of hockey, no other scoring champ has ever been booed by his hometown fans.

Years later, the Canadiens — famous for recognizing their own — bungled Geoffrion's long-overdue jersey retirement celebration. They waited too long.

On March 11, 2006, Boom Boom was not at the Montreal Forum to see his number 5 retired, to hear the waves of applause. Sadly, he passed away from stomach cancer in an Atlanta hospital just five hours before the ceremony.

Had the ceremony been planned for earlier in the season, he would have been able to attend. But the organizers selected the March 11 date because the Rangers were in town, the team Geoffrion had played for and coached after leaving the Habs. What's more, the date chosen also coincided with the 69th anniversary of Howie Morenz's jersey retirement by the Canadiens.

SHORE'S QUIRKS

Many years ago, Don Cherry played four seasons on defence for Springfield of the American Hockey League. There he observed the oddball behaviour of owner/manager/coach Eddie Shore, one of the most bizarre characters in hockey.

Among Cherry's observations were the following:

- Springfield players were instructed by Shore never to tip a cab driver more than 15 cents. As a result, cabbies tried to avoid picking up hockey players.

- At contract time, Shore would grant a player bonus money for scoring 30 goals. But when the player reached 29 goals, he was likely to find himself riding the bench for the rest of the season.

- If one of his goalies flopped to the ice too often in workouts, Shore would get a rope and tie him to the crossbar.

- When Shore needed goaltending help one season, he traded for a player named Smith. When Smith arrived, Shore asked him, "Where are your goal pads?" Smith answered, "Mr. Shore, I'm not a goalie, I'm a left winger."

- One player traded to Springfield arrived in time to see the team working out in a hotel lobby. They were practising dance routines. The player fled.

- Springfield's "Black Aces" were players who were in Shore's doghouse. They practised but seldom played. They were required to paint the arena seats, sell programs at games, make popcorn, and blow up balloons for special events. One day, as punishment for some misdeed, player Roger Cote was told to run around a track across from the arena. "Give me time to get my skates off," he said. "No, leave your skates on," he was told.

And finally, when Cherry was traded to Three Rivers (Trois Rivières), he asked Shore, "Where's Three Rivers?"

"Drive to the Canadian border and turn right," was Shore's reply.

GARBAGE CAN POOR REPLICA OF THE CUP

During their initial NHL season (1974–75), the Washington Capitals shattered a modern-day record for futility with their 8 wins, 67 losses, and 5 ties. In one 11-game stretch, they were shut out five times. They established a record for consecutive losses with 17 and another mark for losses on the road with 37. The team went through three coaches that season — Jim Anderson (54 games), Red Sullivan (19 games), and Milt Schmidt (7 games). When they won a game late in the season, they celebrated by lifting a garbage can high in the air and parading around the dressing room with it — their version of the Stanley Cup. If someone suggested they drink from it, the idea was squashed. In 1992–93, the Ottawa Senators lost one more road game than the Caps to establish a new low mark. During the same season, the San Jose Sharks established a new record for losses with 71.

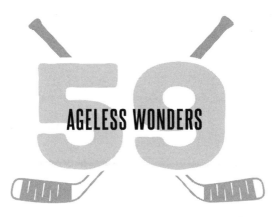

AGELESS WONDERS

Manager Lester Patrick of the New York Rangers had long been retired from hockey as a player when his team faced the Montreal Maroons in a 1929 playoff game. In the second period, Rangers goalie Lorne Chabot was struck in the face by a puck and was rushed to a nearby hospital. Teams had no backup goalies in those days, and when the Maroons vetoed Patrick's plea to use Alec Connell, a splendid goalie with Ottawa, he fumed and said, "All right, I'll take over for Chabot." So he did, and he played well; his team won the game, and a few days later, with Chabot back between the pipes, captured the Stanley Cup. For decades Patrick reigned as the oldest goaltender in NHL history. He was 44 years and 99 days old.

In time, three other netminders erased Patrick's NHL record from the book. Moe Roberts, a trainer with the

Blackhawks, played one period in one game in 1951 at 45 years, 345 days old. Johnny Bower of the Leafs was still a regular goalie at 45 years, 32 days old in 1969, and Gump Worsley was 45 years, 323 days old in 1974.

Jacques Plante can legitimately be crowned as the oldest goalie in pro hockey history, even though he finished his career in the WHA in 1975. By then he was 46 years old. Plante played in the NHL at age 44 years, 78 days — just 21 days shy of Lester Patrick's mark.

Can you name the oldest rookie to play in the NHL? When the league expanded from six to 12 teams in 1967– 68, the St. Louis Blues called up 38-year-old Connie Madigan from the minor leagues. Madigan lasted 25 games and later played Mad Dog Madison in the movie *Slap Shot*.

The oldest player to be drafted by an NHL club was Latvian star Helmut Balderis, age 36, who was drafted by the Minnesota North Stars in the '70s. At 37, he became the oldest player to score his first NHL goal.

Of course, the Grand Old Man of hockey was Gordie Howe, who said farewell to the game in 1980 at 52 years, 11 days old. In 1997, at 69 years of age, Howe suited up for one shift with the Detroit Vipers of the International Hockey League.

Two other ironmen are Chris Chelios and Jaromir Jagr. Chelios played until he was 48 years and 71 days old. And

Jagr walked away at 45 years, 319 days. Jagr is also the oldest player to score a hat trick in the NHL (42 years, 322 days). And he's the only player to be in the Stanley Cup Final both as a teen and in his 40s.

THE YOUNGEST TO PLAY PRO

Bep Guidolin was just 16 years and 11 months old when he played his first NHL game with the Boston Bruins on November 12, 1942 (Toronto 3, Boston 1). But even younger was 14-year-old Doug Bentley Jr., who became the youngest player *outside the NHL* to play a few shifts in a professional hockey game. On March 13, 1966, with permission from the league, Bentley (the coach's son) played in an Eastern Hockey League game between the Knoxville Knights and the Jacksonville Rockets.

HAVE A HOT DOG, GEORGE

When he played for the St. Louis Blues, winger George Morrison spent more time on the bench than he did on the ice. Coach Scotty Bowman didn't seem to care that he'd been a big star in college hockey. In Los Angeles one night, an usher whispered to him, "George, can I have your stick after the game?" Bored and hungry, Morrison replied, "Sneak me a hot dog and a Coke and you can have my stick." Moments later, the usher slipped Morrison the hot dog and the drink. That's when Coach Bowman roared, "Morrison, get out there and kill that penalty!"

Caught by surprise, Morrison knocked the drink off the bench and quickly stuffed the hot dog down the cuff of his hockey glove. But when he leaped on the ice, an opposing player slammed into him and the hot dog flew into the air, mustard and relish sailing in all directions.

Only when he retired did Morrison confess he once carried a hot dog into an NHL game.

A half-eaten one at that!

NOEL PICARD GETS A BIT CONFUSED

Defenceman Noel Picard is prominent in one of hockey's most famous photographs. In the final game of the 1970 Stanley Cup playoffs, he was the St. Louis Blues defenceman who hoisted Bobby Orr in the air just as he scored the Cup-winning goal for the Boston Bruins. The photo of the goal has been reproduced thousands of times.

Noel Picard is also the only NHL player who joined the opposing team in the middle of an NHL game.

One night in Boston, playing on defence for the Blues, he skated to the Boston bench during a line change, leading some to believe he was colour blind. The Bruins' trainer opened the gate for Picard, and the big guy waltzed in and sat down among the Bruins players. When he heard them laughing, he realized where he was. Too embarrassed to wait for the next whistle, he dashed off the Bruins bench and tried to sneak across the ice to the St. Louis bench. What was he thinking? A big guy like him pretending he was invisible? Of course, the referee caught him and gave the Blues a penalty for too many men on the ice. Red Berenson, the Blues' best player at the time, cracked up, laughing so hard that the Blues' coach, a young Scotty Bowman, almost went ballistic. And who could blame him?

THE GAME I NEVER SAW
(EVEN THOUGH I WAS RINKSIDE)

I was hosting the NBC broadcast of a game played at the
ancient Buffalo Memorial Auditorium on an unseasonably
hot May 20 back in 1975. There was no air conditioning in
that barn, folks. The Buffalo Sabres were at home, hosting the
Philadelphia Flyers in Game 3 of the Stanley Cup Final. Prior
to game time, a thick fog began to fill the arena. The result was
a game played like no other, in conditions so bizarre that fans
and players (and I) couldn't see the puck at all. I recall the blur
of uniforms when players scooted behind the net and then
disappeared into the soup. Play was halted every few minutes
while college kids with sheets skated around trying to circulate
air and dissipate the fog in the sweltering building. But their
efforts were in vain. It's a wonder no players were hurt when
they accidentally crashed into each other.

Flyers goaltender Bernie Parent said, "The NHL looked like a bush league that day. There has never been a playoff game in history like that one."

Rene Robert's overtime goal won it for the Sabres 5–4.

The Flyers recovered, however, and when Parent shut out the Sabres 2–0 in Game 6, he paraded the Stanley Cup around the arena — the Buffalo arena.

"The Buffalo fans even chanted my name — 'Bern-ie! Bern-ie!' — just like the Flyers fans did back home. That was nice of them."

WHERE'S THE REF?

Frank Carlin was manager/coach of the Montreal Royals back in the 1940s. One day he told me about playing a game in Boston when the referee appeared to be missing.

"I was worried," Carlin told me, "because I looked all over for the referee and couldn't find him. I found the two linesmen, but there was no referee for the game. When I mentioned his absence to the linesmen, they just laughed and said, 'He's up there' — pointing skyward. Sure enough, high over the ice, sitting in a gondola, was the referee. Somebody figured he'd have a better overall view of things if he was high over the ice in a kind of basket. I swear it was the only time I'd ever seen such a thing. So we played in the only game in which the referee was perched 40 or 50 feet above the action. If he called a lousy penalty, the players below had only the linesmen to argue with. And they would say, 'Don't tell us about it. He's the guy who made the call.' And they'd point skyward again."

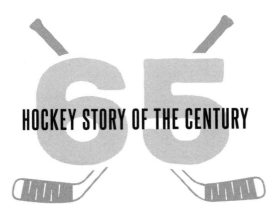

HOCKEY STORY OF THE CENTURY

"The Miracle on Ice" is the name given to a stunning upset at the 1980 Olympics, held in Lake Placid, New York. On February 22, the American hockey team, made up of college players and led by coach Herb Brooks, defeated the Soviet powerhouse, considered the best hockey team in the world, in the medal round. Team USA went on to capture the gold medal by winning their final match over Finland. It was the second gold medal win for a U.S. hockey club. The first was at Squaw Valley, California, in 1960 — another major upset. In the four Olympics that followed the 1960 Games, Soviet teams had won 22 games and lost 2, outscoring the opposition 175–44.

As part of its 100th anniversary celebrations in 2008, the International Ice Hockey Federation chose the Miracle on Ice as the number one international hockey story of the century. But in Canada, it's almost certain Team Canada's win over the Soviets in 1972 — an eight-game series that ended with Paul Henderson's winning goal in Moscow — would garner more votes than the Miracle on Ice.

FIFTY GOALS IN SEVEN GAMES

We all know about Wayne Gretzky's fabulous career in hockey: how he holds dozens of scoring records, and how, as a young phenom, he scored 1,000 goals before he turned 13. But here's an eyewitness account of Wayne's performance in a pee-wee tournament in his hometown of Brantford, Ontario — as told by Vic Symes, who was president of the Brantford Minor Hockey Association at the time.

"I remember vividly one tournament that really emphasized Wayne's determination. He was only 11, and playing in a pee-wee tournament in which his team played seven games. Those in attendance were astonished when he scored 49 goals and was going for an even 50 when he took a penalty at 17:47 of the third period in the final game. Well, he sat quietly in the penalty box, but stormed out with 13 seconds on the clock. He raced after the puck, grabbed it, rushed in, and scored. He reached into the net, picked up the puck, and went to the Brantford bench. Most fans had never seen anything like that in their lives. Imagine scoring 50 goals in one seven-game tournament."

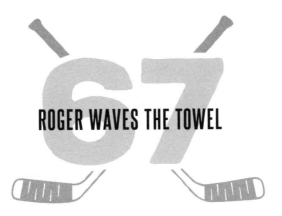

ROGER WAVES THE TOWEL

On a spring night in 1982, Vancouver coach Roger Neilson raised a white towel in a gesture of mock surrender. Towel Power was born.

But our story begins in Quebec City late in the season — Vancouver versus Quebec. The fans began heckling Canucks head coach Harry Neale. When Neale was peppered with debris, he and his players turned on the howling mob.

As a result of the melee, Neale was suspended for the remaining six games of the season. Roger Neilson stepped in to take over coaching duties, and the Canucks went undefeated for the rest of the season.

Neale was smart enough to keep Neilson behind the bench for the playoffs. The Canucks swarmed all over Calgary in the first round. In the next round, they faced the

L.A. Kings, who were coming off a stunning upset over the Edmonton Oilers.

The Kings were hot, but they couldn't cope with Roger Neilson's magic.

The third round was memorable. The Canucks invaded the old Chicago Stadium and emerged with a double-overtime victory in Game 1.

I watched from the *Hockey Night in Canada* booth as the Canucks stumbled in Game 2, dinged with four straight penalties in the second period. The Canucks' Tiger Williams would later accuse referee Bob Myers of making incredibly terrible decisions.

When Myers signalled a fifth penalty against the Canucks, Williams lost his cool. He wanted to "throw every friggin' stick on the ice." But Neilson said, "Watch this." He grabbed a spare stick and threw a white towel around the blade. He lifted it high in Myers's face — a mock surrender. The Chicago mob booed, then roared with laughter.

Neilson's perfect protest won huge support from Vancouver fans watching on television. The Canucks were unbeatable in the next three games as towel-waving fans appeared everywhere.

For Game 3 in Vancouver, it was a sea of white as more than 16,000 rabid fans looked on gleefully when the Canucks edged ahead in the series. The snowstorm was back when the Canucks rolled to another win in Game 4. In the next game, played in Chicago, the Hawks fell again. Late in the match, they tossed in the towel themselves. Goaltender Richard Brodeur's fabulous goaltending and a million towels sent the Canucks into their first ever Stanley Cup Final series.

But alas, the magic in Roger's towels was running out. The New York Islanders seized their third straight Stanley Cup and would come right back with a fourth the next year, becoming the first American team to do so.

Neilson is no longer with us, but his impulsive stick wave, with white towel flapping, will forever be remembered by aging Canucks fans.

MARTY WAS A MIGHTY MITE

Marty St. Louis is small. He says he's five-foot-nine, but that must be with his skates on. Or small stilts. St. Louis was a fabulous scorer in his college hockey days at the University of Vermont. In four seasons there, after becoming an All-American and two-time nominee for the Hobey Baker Award as MVP, St. Louis finished his college career four points shy of the Eastern College Athletic Conference all-time scoring record.

Despite his scoring feats, Marty was ignored by all the NHL teams, and not one of them drafted him. Eventually he signed a free-agent contract with the Calgary Flames, who soon gave up on him. He then signed with the Tampa Bay Lightning for the 2000–2001 season, and that's where he began his rise to stardom. In 2003–4, St. Louis won the

Hart Trophy (MVP), the Art Ross Trophy (scoring leader), the Lester B. Pearson Award (players' choice as MVP, now known as the Ted Lindsay Award), and the Stanley Cup. Not bad for a little fellow from Laval, Quebec, who ignored the people who judged him "too small for the NHL."

BOBBY DID IT ALL

When Bobby Orr retired in November 1978 after a brilliant 12-year career with Boston and Chicago, he had won the Norris Trophy eight times as the NHL's top defenceman, the Hart Trophy three times as league MVP, and the Art Ross Trophy twice as the individual scoring champ. And he did all that despite having at least six operations on his wonky knees. The Hockey Hall of Fame waived the mandatory three-year waiting period for induction and Orr was enshrined in the Hall at age 31, one of only 10 players to get in without having to wait the three years.

How popular was Bobby in Boston? He was named the greatest Boston athlete of all time, ahead of legends like Ted Williams and Bob Cousy. Though perhaps another vote today would have him challenged by Patriots quarterback Tom Brady.

Here are some fascinating facts about the great Bobby Orr: He was the first defenceman to score 30 goals in a season (1969–70), the first defenceman to score 40 goals in a season (1974–75), the first player to register 100 assists in a season (1970–71), and the only defenceman to lead the NHL in scoring twice (in 1969–70 and 1974–75). He is also the only player to win the Art Ross, the Hart, the Norris, and the Conn Smythe trophies in a single season and the only defenceman to collect nine hat tricks.

Orr owns the record for the highest plus/minus in one season (+124 in 1970–71), and he ranks second overall for most goals by a defenceman in one season with 46 (Paul Coffey had 48 in 1985–86).

Sadly, Orr played only 657 NHL games, fewer than most of the greats, but he compiled stunning stats in that time — 270 goals and 645 assists for a total of 915 points. He averaged 1.393 points per game — fifth best among all players and highest for a defenceman. For a non-forward to average the fifth highest points per game of all time is astonishing.

STILL FULL OF FIRE — AT 84

"Guys like me — hockey players — we're the dumbest bunch of athletes in the world," Aurel Joliat stated when we shared a microphone in Ottawa one day. Columnist Earl McRae would write a full article about the energetic Joliat, then 84, beginning with that quote. Joliat added, "We never got paid much, and most of us never had the sense to save much."

Joliat went on to reminisce about his pioneering days in the NHL and his career with the Canadiens. Born in Ottawa, he played from 1922 to 1938 and retired as the highest-scoring left winger in history at the time, with 270 goals.

Joliat was a tough little guy. He proved that as a teen-ager when he fell off a roof, tumbled head over heels to the ground, and landed on his back. He played 13 seasons in the NHL with two displaced vertebrae, which caused him great pain and forced him to wear an elaborate truss. He was tough enough to become a star kicker with his hometown Ottawa Rough Riders, until a broken leg forced him to give up football.

"For a little runt, sure I was tough enough," he said. "But that mule-headed sonofabitch Eddie Shore was maybe tougher. He was the meanest opponent I ever tangled with. I was rushin' up the ice at the Forum one night when my lights went out. Shore hit me — *wham!* — and almost killed me. I was what, 130 pounds, and he musta been 190. They were carryin' me off in a lot of pain when I look around, and there's Shore leading a fancy rush. Damn him! I leaped over the boards and nailed the big bugger with a flyin' tackle. Hit him so hard he was out cold on the ice. He had it comin', I'd say."

Joliat played on three Stanley Cup–winning teams. He was named league MVP in 1934. In 1985, 60 years after he played in the opening game at the Montreal Forum, he was invited back as an honorary member of the Canadiens' "Dream Team." At the age of 83, he delighted the fans with an energetic display of skating and stickhandling, ending his routine with a mighty pratfall over a red carpet he hadn't noticed. "The ghost of Eddie Shore must have put that damn rug in front of me," he told Earl McRae.

In his 70s, Joliat was invited to Boston for a reunion of living hockey legends. Among the other celebs was Punch Broadbent, another tough customer who'd often traded blows and stick jabs with Joliat.

In the pressroom prior to the dinner, the two old-timers got embroiled in an argument over some long-ago incident. After punches were thrown and a dandy fight broke out, NHL president Clarence Campbell intervened and told them they were no longer invited to the dinner.

Not long after the Boston shenanigans, Joliat told McRae he'd like to make a comeback in the NHL. "If a team made me a good offer, I'd come back," he said, straight-faced. "I'd show 'em."

"How long do you think you'd last out there?" McRae asked.

"About five minutes."

"Only five minutes a game?"

"Game, hell — five minutes a *shift*!"

MARIO THE MAGNIFICENT

Has an NHL rookie ever scored a goal in his first game? On his first shot? On his first shift? Mario Lemieux did.

A rookie with the Pittsburgh Penguins in 1984–85, Lemieux, the most prolific scorer in Quebec Major Junior Hockey League history, in his initial NHL season, scored 43 goals and racked up 100 points, earning him the Calder Trophy as rookie of the year. In midseason, Mario was also named MVP of the All-Star Game.

Lemieux went on to enjoy a fabulous career, one that rivalled that of Wayne Gretzky. He helped bring two Stanley Cups to Pittsburgh and, in retirement — can you believe it? — he bought the team. He retired as the NHL's seventh-highest-ranked career scorer with 690 goals and 1,033 assists, averaging 0.754 goals per game, behind only Mike Bossy (0.762).

He created a "first" as a player by scoring five goals in a game in five different ways: an even-strength goal, a power-play goal, a short-handed goal, a penalty-shot goal, and an empty-net goal.

In 1999, with the Penguins owing him millions, he took over the bankrupt club, and he is currently the team's principal owner and chairman. Under his leadership, the Penguins won Stanley Cups in 2009, 2016, and 2017. Lemieux is the only man to have his name on the Cup as both a player and an owner.

CUP CUP AND AWAY

In 1892, Canada's governor general, Lord Stanley of Preston, was living in Ottawa. As the Queen's representative, he was highly respected. Ottawa hockey fans liked him because he became a big fan of the sport and supported the city's hockey club.

Two of his sons, Algernon and Arthur, became skilled players. They said to him one day, "Dad, do you know there's no trophy awarded to the league champions? We think you should donate one. When your term here in Canada is over and we all go back to England, people will remember you for the trophy you left behind."

Lord Stanley must have agreed because, not long after, a beautiful silver bowl about the size of a football was in his hands.

Although he hoped the Ottawa team would be the first recipient of the new trophy that bore his name, in the spring of 1894, a Montreal team was the winningest club.

Lord Stanley was not even there to present the Cup, as he'd been recalled to England some time earlier. The presentation was instead made by league officials.

So Lord Stanley, poor fellow, never got to see a Stanley Cup playoff game; nor did he get to shake the hands of the first winners from the Montreal Amateur Athletic Association. But his little silver bowl soon became hugely popular from coast to coast. Any respectable team was allowed to challenge for it, and soon teams from across the nation were eager to capture the gleaming trophy.

Lord Stanley is the only individual in the Hockey Hall of Fame who never gained fame as a player, coach, referee, or builder.

FORREST FACES FASCINATING CHALLENGE

Imagine this: You're a young goaltender with a chance to play for the Stanley Cup. Your parents have given you permission to go, even though you're just 17. But getting to the arena would be a huge challenge. It's 4,000 miles away. There are no cars, no buses, and no planes. The nearest railway station is 350 miles away. Plus it's December in the Far North — and the weather is about to turn nasty.

That was the challenge facing young Albert Forrest and his teammates on December 19, 1904, when they set off from Dawson City in the Yukon for Ottawa, where a powerful club, the Ottawa Silver Seven, was waiting for them.

Forrest and his teammates started out a week before Christmas, some on foot, some on bicycles. They figured it would take a month to get there, but that was just a guess.

If it took longer, the best-of-three series for the Stanley Cup could be cancelled.

The epic story of the marathon trip made by the Dawson City team, nicknamed the Nuggets, had everything but a happy ending. The team left Dawson City in good spirits. When the bicycles broke down in the deep snow, it has been said that the players hitched rides on passing dog-sleds. Within a few days, they had arrived in Whitehorse. From there, they travelled by narrow-gauge railway to Skagway, located on the coast of Alaska, where, after waiting five days for a ship to arrive, they climbed aboard a tramp streamer headed for Seattle, Washington. When they landed in Seattle, they promptly boarded a train headed north to Vancouver. From there, another train carried them across the country to Ottawa.

When they climbed down from the train on January 12, 1905, they had covered close to 4,000 miles in 24 days. Fatigued, they pleaded for a postponement of the best-of-three Cup series. "Let us get our skating legs back," they pleaded.

"Sorry. Can't be done," declared the Ottawa manager. "The ice time has been booked, the tickets sold. We'll play tomorrow night."

Predictably, Ottawa whipped the weary challengers by scores of 9–2 and 23–2. It remains the most one-sided series in Stanley Cup history. In the second game, Ottawa star

"One-Eyed" Frank McGee scored 14 goals against young Forrest, a record that still stands.

Not only was Forrest the youngest goalie ever to play for the Cup, he'll be forever listed as the one with the worst goals-against record in Cup history. Poor kid.

But the young goalkeeper was praised in the Ottawa newspapers, with one reporter writing, "Forrest was indeed a marvel. But for him, the score in the series would have been double what it was. Two Ottawa goals were questionable and three others were scored despite being offside." Another wrote: "Dawson never had a chance. It was like putting a sugar bun in the hands of a small boy."

McGee has been inducted into the Hockey Hall of Fame; Albert Forrest has not.

SMALL-TOWN VICTORS

The smallest community to win the Stanley Cup was Kenora, Ontario. Kenora, originally known as Rat Portage, was a town of only a few hundred people, but the team owner imported some wonderful players.

In January 1907, the Kenora Thistles captured the Cup by beating the Montreal Wanderers 4–2 and 8–6 at Montreal. Led by Tom Phillips, who scored seven goals in the two-game series, the Thistles skated the Wanderers into the ice.

The Montreal team was stunned by the loss, as they had gone undefeated in 10 games, and in each of those games had averaged more than 10 goals. Before the 1907 season was over, they journeyed to Kenora and won back the Cup, outscoring the Thistles 12–8 over two games.

When the Cup trustees insisted that the second series of games be played on a larger ice surface in Winnipeg, the Stanley Cup narrowly missed ending up at the bottom of a lake. An irate Kenora official threatened to throw it into the Lake of the Woods if the games weren't played in Kenora.

HEY, MOM, YOUR NAME'S ON THE CUP!

Once the coveted trophy is captured, all winning players are eager to have their names engraved on the Cup. But at least one team didn't wait for a professional engraver to do his job. The players instead used a metal instrument to scratch their names into it. One player even scratched his infant son's name into it; another put his mother's name on it.

Back then, Cup winners often showed little respect for the trophy. For example, while walking home from a championship game, with the first stop being a tavern, the Ottawa champs, on a dare, drop-kicked the Cup into the Rideau Canal. Ker-plunk! Into the slush and ice it went.

"It's too dark to climb down there and get it," said one of the culprits. "We'll come back tomorrow and fetch it."

And that's what they did.

I talked to Hall of Fame player King Clancy about the early adventures of the Stanley Cup. He admitted that "pioneer players like me should have shown more respect. It sat in my house in Ottawa one summer and my friends treated it like an ashtray. Cigar butts were left in it … maybe some chewing gum. Ottawa's Alf Smith stuffed it in a closet one summer and then forgot where he'd put it when it came time to hand it over to another team."

MUD'S MARKER ENDS MARATHON GAME

On March 24, 1936, the Detroit Red Wings and the Montreal Maroons met in the first round of the Stanley Cup playoffs. The Wings' Norm Smith and Maroons' Lorne Chabot were the opposing goaltenders when the teams faced off at the Montreal Forum. But many in the crowd would not be around for the end of the match; most would be back home, fast asleep.

That's because Detroit's Mud Bruneteau scored the game's only goal — at 2:25 a.m., at 16:30 of the *sixth* overtime period.

Norm Smith recorded the shutout in the longest NHL game ever played — 176 minutes and 30 seconds. The *Guinness Book of World Records* sanctioned the 92 saves Smith made in the game as a world record. Smith's NHL career wasn't long — it lasted only 198 games — but over that time, he won a Vezina Trophy and two Stanley Cups. And he'll always be remembered as the winning goalie in the longest game ever played.

A MAGIC MOMENT FOR MOORE

His season over, minor-league goaltender Alfie Moore was sitting in a Toronto tavern on the afternoon of April 5, 1938. He'd soon go home and listen to Foster Hewitt's radio broadcast of the Toronto-Chicago Stanley Cup playoff game that night. Moore had given up all hope of getting a ticket to the game. He looked up and saw two Blackhawks stars, Johnny Gottselig and Paul Thompson, barge into the tavern, looking around. They were looking for him.

They rushed over and said, "Come with us, Alfie. We're taking you to Maple Leaf Gardens. You're going to be the Chicago goalie tonight."

The Blackhawks, with just 14 wins in the regular season that year, had stunned the Montreal Canadiens and New York Americans in a pair of best-of-three series in the 1938 playoffs. Now they faced Toronto in the finals, but they had little chance of winning. Their star goalie, Mike Karakas, had a broken toe, and it was so badly swollen that his foot wouldn't squeeze into the boot of his skate.

Bill Stewart, the Hawks' coach, pleaded with Leafs owner Conn Smythe to let him employ Davey Kerr, a New York Rangers regular, as a substitute, but Smythe just laughed. "Forget about Kerr. He's one of the best. But I'll let you use a minor-leaguer named Alfie Moore. That is, if you can find him."

The search party tracked down Moore, hustled him to the Gardens, found some goaltending gear for him, and pulled a Chicago jersey over his head.

Moore stopped a few pucks in the pre-game warm-up and then pronounced himself ready. But he looked shaky and gave up a goal on the first shot he faced.

Moore took a deep breath, pulled himself together, and was the picture of composure as he blanked the Leafs the rest of the way. The Hawks won the game 3–1. His new teammates skated over and pounded Moore on the back and pumped his hand. As he skated off the ice, the happy goal-tender couldn't resist thumbing his nose at Conn Smythe.

Perhaps it was the thumb to the nose that outraged Smythe, and he refused to allow the Hawks to use Moore in Game 2 of the series. Paul Goodman, a Hawks farm-hand, replaced him, and Toronto won 5–1. Karakas was back in goal for Game 3 in Chicago and played brilliantly, backing the Hawks to 2–1 and 4–1 wins, as the Cinderella Blackhawks captured the Stanley Cup.

The grateful Hawks paid Moore $300 (double what he'd asked for) and threw in a gold watch, a memento he treasured long after his one-shot Stanley Cup heroics were history. "As it turned out, I played in only 21 regular-season games in my entire NHL career, none of them with Chicago. Then, in the only game I played as a Hawk, I got my name engraved on the Stanley Cup. Who'd have believed that would ever happen?"

WHAT A COMEBACK!

In the 1941 Stanley Cup Final, with his team leading Toronto 3–1 in the series, Detroit manager Jack Adams jumped on the ice at the end of Game 4 and tried to rough up the referee. If one of his players had done it, Adams would have rebuked him, ordered him to get to the dressing room, and probably fined him for taking a stupid penalty. But Adams, who prided himself on being a leader and a great coach, lost his composure and went after the referee. He came just short of punching him in the nose. Of course he was suspended indefinitely, and it marked a turning point in the series. His team sagged, and Toronto regrouped, won three in a row, and captured the Stanley Cup in what has been called "hockey's greatest comeback."

DON'T LOSE THOSE GLOVES, MARCEL

Marcel Bonin played on four Stanley Cup–winning teams, one in Detroit and three with the Montreal Canadiens. One year, 1959, hoping to change his scoring luck, Bonin borrowed a pair of Rocket Richard's old gloves. "Maybe they'll help me get out of my slump," he told Richard.

Over the next eight games, Bonin scored eight goals. In the playoffs, he scored 11 goals and had 15 points in 10 games.

He would play in 39 other playoff games and collect just a single goal.

If there'd been a Conn Smythe Trophy back then, Bonin would have captured it in '59.

Bonin is the only hockey player known to wrestle bears for a living. When he was a teenager, he made a few bucks going from town to town in Quebec, following the Barnum & Bailey circus. When the ringmaster called for volunteers to wrestle a bear, Bonin was quick to throw his arm up and enter the ring.

One day Bonin told me how he got to be friends with that old bear.

"I was a pretty tough kid, so I jumped in that ring and wrestled that bear. I didn't put him down but you could call the match a draw, eh. Okay, the bear he wore a muzzle and he had no claws, but still everybody cheered and talked about how this kid, Marcel Bonin — only 16 — fought the big bear. My name was in all the papers; the bear's name was never mentioned.

"I wrestled that bear in lots of towns. But I was no dummy, eh. I went to that bear in the morning and fed him and soon we were good pals, eh. And that's how I got to be known as Bonin the Bear Wrestler."

YOU WON'T LAST 20 GAMES, KELLY

For years I watched one of the best players in the world play for the Toronto Maple Leafs — Red Kelly. Red was also the first player I ever interviewed on network hockey, on CBS in 1960, the year he was traded — not to the Leafs, but to the New York Rangers.

"I had a cracked ankle in 1959," Red told me. "It still bothered me the following season, and Jack Adams, the Detroit manager, figured I was on my last legs. Suddenly I found out I'd been traded to New York — just like that. The next day I told Mr. Adams I wasn't going to move to New York. He glared at me and said hotly, 'Well, Red, you have to go. You've been traded. Don't you get it?' Well, I did get it. And I didn't like it. So I walked out.

"NHL president Clarence Campbell phoned me immediately and threatened me. He said, 'Red, you must go to New York. If you don't, you'll be blackballed by the NHL — forever.' But I refused to go, so the deal was nullified.

"Then King Clancy of the Leafs called and said, 'Look, Red, come to Toronto. Mr. Imlach would like to talk to you.' So I flew to Toronto and talked to Punch Imlach about the possibility of me playing for Toronto. Punch and I finally made a deal. Imlach sent Detroit a player for me — Marc Rheaume.

"What a wonderful way to finish my career. I played on three Stanley Cup winners as a Leaf, and then a fourth in 1967, when everybody said the Leafs were too old to beat Montreal. Well, we were old, but we beat Montreal in six games, with Johnny Bower and Terry Sawchuk giving us the goaltending we needed.

"For three of those seasons, I had another job. I served as a Member of Parliament. In one election I won by 17,000 votes, beating out a young lawyer named Alan Eagleson.

"After we won the Cup in '64, Bob Baun and I were both on the limp. He had scored a dramatic goal to win a crucial game in Detroit while playing on a broken leg.

"There was no time for partying for either of us. I went straight home and rose early and left for my job in Ottawa. Harold Ballard, the Leafs owner, came to my house that morning. He had the Stanley Cup with him and a photographer in tow.

"When my wife, Andra, told him I wasn't home, Ballard said, 'Well, get your kids together around the Cup and we'll take some photos.' When the photographer had Andra put our baby son, Conn, in the bowl of the Stanley Cup, he promptly took a poop. I think about that and smile every year when I see fellows drinking from it."

Conn Kelly overheard the remark and said, "Dad, all the great things you accomplished in your life and that's the best story you can come up with?"

On the *Hockey News* list of hockey's top 100 players, Red Kelly is listed at number 22. He played in 1,316 games, almost 1,300 more than the mere 20 a scout had predicted for him. He was inducted into the Hockey Hall of Fame in 1969. Recently, the Red Wings retired Kelly's famous number 4, something his old manager Jack Adams would never have done.

AND THE OSCAR GOES TO ...

When the Edmonton Oilers faced off against the New York Islanders in the1983 Stanley Cup Final, Islanders goaltender Billy Smith was the man of the moment, wielding a heavy stick.

In Game 1, Smith slashed Oiler Glenn Anderson across the knee. In Game 2, he slashed at Wayne Gretzky when the league's top scorer came out from behind the net. In Game 4, he collided with Anderson in his crease and then tumbled to the ice, writhing in pain. The referee tossed Anderson for five minutes. Smith promptly jumped up, smiling. The Isles won the series in four games, and Smith admitted on *Hockey Night in Canada* he'd taken a dive. His confession was heard by NHL president John Ziegler, who'd just handed him the Conn Smythe Trophy. Smith said, "Sure, I planned the dive.

I rolled around on the ice like Gretzky did when I hit him. He [lay] down and cried. Two can play at that game."

Smith's public admission of his deceit infuriated many TV viewers. Even so, his critics had to agree his remarkable puck-stopping had been a big factor in the Isles' win.

WATCH YOUR MOUTH, COACH

In 1982–83, rookie coach Orval Tessier guided the Chicago Blackhawks from 30 wins and 72 points to 47 wins and 104 points and a first-place finish in their division — a stunning improvement. Tessier would be named coach of the year.

But his career took a sudden nosedive in the play-offs. The Blackhawks met the Edmonton Oilers in the conference final and were chased in four straight games. Livid with rage after suffering through 8–4 and 8–2 losses, Tessier told the media, "My players need 18 heart transplants."

Those few ill-chosen words would cost Tessier all the respect he'd earned that season. Reporters began calling him "Mount Orval" and "Lava Lips."

In the next season and a half, the Hawks plunged from 104 points to 68 points. Mount Orval was fired and never got a second chance to coach in the NHL.

BOURQUE'S LONG WAIT

It took 22 seasons and 214 playoff games before Colorado Avalanche defenceman Ray Bourque was able to lift the Stanley Cup over his head and shout, "I didn't think this day would ever come!"

Bourque's memorable day came on June 9, 2001, in Denver, when the Colorado Avalanche captured the Stanley Cup with a 3–1 defeat of the New Jersey Devils in Game 7. Avalanche captain Joe Sakic, in an unselfish act, passed the Stanley Cup to Bourque first for the traditional trophy skate around the arena, breaking a hockey tradition that has the team captain leading the parade.

For a long time, Ray Bourque and Paul Coffey jousted for the title of highest-scoring defenceman in history. Bourque ended his career with 410 goals and 1,579 points.

Coffey was a close second, with 396 goals and 1,531 points. How long will it take for another high-scoring defenceman to match or surpass those numbers?

Bourque spent all but the last few months of his Hall of Fame career as a Boston Bruin.

THE MIRACLE ON MANCHESTER

When I asked Don Cherry and Bob Cole to name the single greatest playoff game they ever worked together for *Hockey Night in Canada*, they both agreed that one in 1982 stood out above all others. The night the L.A. Kings pulled off an upset so stunning it will be forever remembered as "the Miracle on Manchester."

The Kings' arena, the Forum, was located on Manchester Boulevard. Fans everywhere rubbed their eyes in disbelief when the lowly Kings, 17th-place finishers, eliminated the powerful second-place Edmonton Oilers in the first play-off round. The teams set a record of 18 goals in the opener, which was won by the Kings 10–8.

Game 3 on April 10, 1982, produced one of the most incredible endings in NHL history. Wayne Gretzky dazzled in pacing the Oilers to a commanding 5–0 lead after two periods. Kings fans resigned themselves to a blowout loss. Cherry recalls the Oilers taunting the Kings for their ineptness.

But the Kings bounced back with an unbelievable comeback, tying the score on a goal by left winger Steve Bozek at 19:55 of the third period to send the game into overtime. At 2:35 into the extra period, Kings left winger Daryl Evans fired a slapshot off the faceoff, beating Oilers goalie Grant Fuhr to give the Kings a stunning come-from-behind 6–5 overtime victory.

In regular-season play, the Kings had won only 24 games to the Oilers' 48. The Kings went on to topple Gretzky and the Oilers from the playoffs, capturing the series three games to two. Oilers fans were livid, and sports columnist Terry Jones roasted the hometown team in the *Edmonton Journal*: "From today until they've won a playoff series again, they are weak-kneed wimps who thought they were God's gift to the NHL but found out they were nothing but adolescent, front-running, goodtime Charlies who couldn't handle any adversity."

RAW RECRUIT BECOMES PLAYOFF MVP

In three seasons of university hockey at Cornell, Toronto native Ken Dryden had a near-perfect record — 76 wins in 83 games — and was named an All-American goalie. The tall young goaltender had been drafted by the Boston Bruins in 1964, but his pro rights were traded to Montreal for a couple of other young players (neither of whom ever played a shift in the NHL).

In 1970–71, Dryden broke into pro hockey with the Canadiens' farm team in Halifax. Late that season, the Habs called him up and gave him a half-dozen starts. He won them all. One night at the Montreal Forum, on March 20, 1971, he and his brother Dave (a Buffalo goalie) made hockey history when they played against each other. Ken skated off with the win.

The 1971 playoffs began with the Canadiens pitted against the powerful Boston Bruins, led by superstars Bobby Orr and Phil Esposito. Boston had finished with 24 more points than the Habs over the season. So, the Bruins were stunned when Coach Scotty Bowman started Dryden — a raw rookie — in goal for Montreal in Game 1. Had Bowman lost his mind?

It was no surprise when Boston took the opener 3–1, and in Game 2, the Bruins raced out to a 5–1 lead. Suddenly, the Canadiens began to fight back. They scored goal after goal to take a 7–5 lead. But the Bruins regrouped and launched a third-period assault on Dryden.

The lanky goaltender was ready for the attack. He played magnificent hockey, and when the final buzzer sounded, he'd won his first playoff game. Throughout the series, Dryden continued to frustrate the Bruins, eventually eliminating them in seven games. Esposito, with a record 76 goals during the regular season, was held to just three in the series.

The Canadiens went on to eliminate the Chicago Blackhawks in the final series for the Stanley Cup. Once again, Dryden played a key role in the victory. At season's end he was awarded the Conn Smythe Trophy as playoff MVP, a remarkable achievement for an inexperienced newcomer.

The following season, he continued to play brilliantly, and because he had not played in 25 games in 1971, he was still officially considered a rookie. It was no surprise when he skated off with the Calder Trophy as the league's top freshman in 1972. No other player in history had been a playoff MVP one season and a rookie award winner the next.

Dryden went on to win 258 games for Montreal while losing only 57. His .758 winning percentage is the best in NHL history. He helped the Habs win six Stanley Cups and starred for Team Canada in 1972. Ken Dryden was inducted into the Hockey Hall of Fame in 1983. After his NHL career ended, he became president of the Toronto Maple Leafs and a Member of Parliament. His book *The Game* is regarded by many as the best hockey book ever written.

THE LAST LAUGH

When the Montreal Canadiens beat the Calgary Flames to win the Stanley Cup in 1986, rookie goalie Patrick Roy was the hero of the series and the Conn Smythe Trophy winner. Roy, who talked to his goalposts during games, became the first rookie in 31 years to chalk up a shutout in the final series. But while the Habs were praising Roy and celebrating their Cup win in Calgary, things turned ugly back in Montreal. The celebration turned into a riot. Fans broke windows, overturned cars, and looted stores in the downtown area. They lit a huge bonfire, and when a fire truck arrived, they attacked it. A riot squad eventually restored order.

Years later, things got ugly again, this time during a December 1995 game in Montreal.

First-year Montreal coach Mario Tremblay let Roy suffer through a game in which he was losing badly. It appeared that Tremblay was being mean spirited, as he and Roy had argued over an issue before the game. When he was finally pulled from the game, Roy stormed off the ice and confronted team president Ron Corey, declaring that he would never again play for the Canadiens. He was suspended, then almost immediately traded to the Colorado Avalanche, where he went on to win a pair of Stanley Cups. Leaving Roy in goal to be tormented by the crowd that night was not one of Tremblay's best coaching decisions.

Patrick Roy would go on to a record-setting Hall of Fame career.

A PRE-GAME BRAWL IN MONTREAL

In the 1980s, brawls were common whenever the Philadelphia Flyers played the Montreal Canadiens. In Game 6 of a 1987 playoff series at the Montreal Forum, an astonishing pre-game brawl broke out — after the warm-up.

The Habs had a ritual of shooting the puck into their opponent's empty net when the warm-up ended. On this night, Flyers tough guy Ed Hospodar and backup goalie Chico Resch were determined to stop them. When the Habs' Shayne Corson and Claude Lemieux moved in to take the empty-net shot, Hospodar rushed over and hooked Corson while Resch threw his goal stick to block the shot. That did it! Within seconds, players from both clubs were involved in a battle that lasted 10 minutes.

Following the game, NHL executive vice-president Brian O'Neill assessed fines totalling $24,000 to the players involved in the fight, and Hospodar was suspended for the balance of the playoffs.

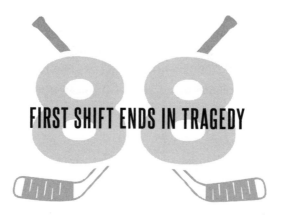

FIRST SHIFT ENDS IN TRAGEDY

One would think it impossible for a hockey player to play only 11 seconds for his team yet have his jersey number retired. But that's just what happened to a Boston University player by the name of Travis Roy. On October 20, 1995, Roy took his first shift in his first game. The 20-year-old freshman player crashed headfirst into the boards at the 11-second mark. Rushed to hospital, Roy underwent seven hours of spinal surgery, but the surgeons had grim news: Roy would never regain the use of his arms or legs.

Today, Roy is in demand as a motivational speaker, and he has established a foundation for spinal cord injury research. Since 1997, the Travis Roy Foundation has distributed more than $9 million in individual grants and to research projects and rehabilitation institutions across North America. He is the only Boston University player to have his jersey number retired, to write an autobiography, and to have an arena named after him.

STICKING IT TO MCSORLEY

The 1993 Stanley Cup Final between the Canadiens and the Kings will long be remembered for the famous Marty McSorley stick measurement in Game 2, which was a turning point in the series. Montreal coach Jacques Demers gambled that the Kings' McSorley was using an illegal stick and called for a measurement. The stick was found to be clearly illegal and McSorley was penalized. The Habs, who were trailing 2–1 at the time, scored the tying goal on the ensuing power play.

Montreal defenceman Eric Desjardins, who scored the power-play goal to force overtime, then scored his third goal of the game 51 seconds into the extra period, becoming the first and only defenceman to collect a hat trick in a Cup Final.

The Habs went on to win the next three games and skated off with their 24th Stanley Cup. The end of that season marked the 100th anniversary of the first awarding of Lord Stanley's Cup in 1893. The Canadiens of 1992–93 are the last Stanley Cup champions to be composed entirely of players born in North America, and they were the last Canadian team to capture the Cup.

There were reports at the time that a Montreal Forum employee assigned to the Kings' locker room moved the Kings' portable stick rack to the door of the Montreal locker room for a few minutes, allowing a Demers assistant to closely examine McSorley's sticks and report back to the coach. Demers said, "That did not happen. Guy Carbonneau spotted it during play."

CAREY PRICE MEETS BRANTFORD BOY

When 11-year-old Anderson Whitehead met his hockey hero, Carey Price, he got more than a handshake and an autograph — he got a hug that brought tears to his eyes. It was the kind of hug his mother used to give him. And his encounter with his goaltending hero was a promise, a gift from his mother, who had passed away from cancer before she could deliver on that promise.

Anderson's family stepped in and helped fulfill it. They arranged for a trip from Brantford to Toronto and then to the Scotiabank Arena. They were allowed to watch the Canadiens' morning skate prior to their game that night with the Leafs. They also got tickets for the game.

At the end of the practice, Carey Price approached Anderson with some gifts in hand. First, he leaned over, like a big brother would, and gave Anderson a huge hug and whispered in his ear, "Everything will be all right."

"Oh my, is Carey really coming over to talk to me?" Anderson remembers asking. There's a video of the meeting, which millions on social media would see. There's the hug, the pair speaking quietly, the gifts of two signed goalie sticks and a souvenir stick, and Price signing Anderson's Montreal jersey. He's obviously in no rush.

Family members and others standing nearby had tears in their eyes. Kevin Whitehead, Anderson's dad, said to his son later, "Can you believe your dream just came true?"

Price declined to speak with reporters after the practice — a good thing — but Habs player Victor Mete said, "Everyone kinda teared up when they saw it. It's really impressive how a guy like that can make someone's day or someone's life. It was pretty cool to see."

MARCHESSAULT FINALLY MAKES IT

MARCHESSAULT is a tough fit on the back of an NHL jersey. And the name Audy-Marchessault is even tighter.

So Jonathan Audy-Marchessault, future hockey star with the Vegas Golden Knights, discarded the *Audy* part of his name while climbing the hockey ladder — not so much for jersey space, but because he didn't want to saddle his newborn daughter with such a lengthy moniker.

What surprises Marchessault's many fans is how long it took him to blossom in professional hockey.

In 2010–11, he was a teenage star in the Quebec junior league, playing for Coach Patrick Roy, the Hall of Fame goaltender. Marchessault was named the Quebec Remparts' player of the year and was a First-Team All-Star. So how come not a single NHL team wanted him?

When he went undrafted on June 23, 2011, he assumed it was because he was a small player, so he decided to prove his critics wrong. He began by signing with the Connecticut Whale in the American Hockey League, where he led the club with 64 points.

As a free agent, he moved on to the Columbus Blue Jackets' AHL affiliate in Springfield and became a First-Team All-Star.

For the 2013–14 season, now with the Blue Jackets, Marchessault dropped *Audy* from his last name, then found himself traded to the Tampa Bay Lightning, who promptly sent him to their Syracuse farm team in the AHL. He didn't sulk or get depressed about the move; he scored 64 points in 64 games.

After three seasons with the Lightning organization, Marchessault left as a free agent and signed with the Florida Panthers. In 2016–17, his first full NHL season, he led the Panthers with 30 goals and 51 points in 75 games. But that wasn't his final destination. Real opportunity and big money awaited him with a brand-new franchise.

On June 21, 2017, Marchessault was selected by the Vegas Golden Knights in the 2017 NHL Expansion Draft. He played a huge role in the Knights' amazing first season. One sparkling performance after another led to contract talks, and on January 3, 2018, the elite left winger signed a six-year, $30 million extension with the Golden Knights.

There was one game Marchessault will never forget. On the night the Golden Knights clinched the NHL's Pacific Division title, the team retired a special jersey — number 58 — and raised a banner with the names of the 58 people killed in the October 1 concert shooting on the Las Vegas Strip. In a pre-game ceremony, the black-and-gold VEGAS STRONG banner was lifted to the rafters at T-Mobile Arena, following a video tribute that was emotional and powerful.

Marchessault would go on to tally 75 points in the regular season and 21 points in the Stanley Cup playoffs as the Golden Knights reached the Stanley Cup Final in their stunning inaugural season.

BROCK BOESER A SURVIVOR

In June 2015, when Brock Boeser was drafted by the Vancouver Canucks inside the BB&T Center in South Florida, he was thinking of his father, Duke, who had nearly died in a car accident when Brock was a high school freshman. His dad was also battling Parkinson's disease.

And Brock was also thinking of his close friend Ty Alyea, who was killed in a car crash that had rocked his Minnesota community of Burnsville months earlier, an accident that left another friend critically injured.

And Brock was thinking about his grandfather, Bob, who had died hours before Brock played a game for Waterloo of the United States Hockey League.

Brock had a lot of sad memories on his mind on a day that should have been one of the happiest of his young life.

He'd played all season for his four pals involved in the car crash — writing the names of Alyea, Cole Borchardt, Matthew Berger, and Tylan Procko on the hockey sticks he used.

His mother, Laurie, said, "Brock had a lot of stuff to deal with. Some very good stuff and some really heavy stuff for a young guy."

In his rookie NHL season (2017–18) Brock led the Canucks in scoring with 29 goals and 55 points in just 62 games, winning praise from just about everyone.

Canucks legend Henrik Sedin called him "the most natural goal scorer I've ever played with."

That season, Brock was selected for the All-Star Game, which was held in January, where he became the first rookie to win MVP honours and $675,000 in prize money — more than two-thirds of his salary. He also won a new electric car, which he gave to his sister, Jessica.

His second season ended prematurely (69 games, 56 points) when a collision with a bench door caused a back injury that sent him to hospital. The injury — and the abnormal number of disasters and health problems among family members and close friends — had him contemplating the risks of playing hockey. "Before my back problems, I'd never think about serious injuries. I mean, career-ending injuries are rare. But now, I think about them a lot."

But Brock has learned much about the vagaries of life — and how to cope with them — from his parents. "I learned strength from my dad. How much he fights. And how he's always smiling, cracking jokes with people, even with everything he has to go through…. And if we didn't have my mom, I don't know how we'd get by. She literally holds everything together."

Back in 2016, a young girl named Baylee Bjorge, who was born with Down's syndrome, reached out to the Canucks' future star via Instagram and invited him to her prom — as her date. Boeser accepted her offer. Baylee's mother said that Brock made her daughter's prom night the "best night of her young life."

GUMP'S GIFT OF GAB

Hall of Fame goaltender Lorne "Gump" Worsley was always a delight to talk to. He had so many interesting hockey stories. One day he shared with me two memories — one good, one bad.

He began with the good.

"When I was with the Rangers, playing against Detroit and big Gordie one night, I fell on my backside while the puck popped high in the air. It came down and landed squarely on my bare face. No goalie masks in those days. And who do I see lookin' down at me, his stick poised for a rebound? Yeah, Mr. Hockey, Gordie Howe.

"He could have torn my kisser apart if he'd shot," said Gump. "So I closed my eyes and gritted my teeth. When I looked up again, he'd eased the puck off my face and tucked it underneath me while the ref blew the play dead. Funny how you don't forget things like that."

And the bad?

"Yeah, my fear of flying. I hated planes," he said. "I was on a flight once when there was so much turbulence the meals jumped off the trays and stained our clothes. A flight attendant came by and promised that the airline would pay for the cleaning of all jackets and slacks. I said to her, 'That's great. What about my shorts?'"

FIND ANOTHER SEAT, PAL!

Bob "Hound Dog" Kelly was one of the more entertaining Philadelphia Flyers. A member of two Stanley Cup–winning teams in the mid-1970s, he scored the winning goal in the sixth game of the 1975 final against Buffalo.

Kelly was interviewed on NBC after the game and then fought his way back to the dressing room, pushing aside media types and autograph-seekers. In the crowded dressing room, he saw a small middle-aged man sitting in front of his locker.

"Hey, old man," he growled. "Get the fuck out of my locker."

The little man jumped up and moved away.

"Who the hell was that?" Kelly asked, still irritated.

"Oh, that's the governor of Pennsylvania, Bob. You sure made him jump."

GORDIE HOWE'S CLOSE CALL

Gordie Howe blossomed into a hockey superstar during the 1949–50 NHL season, finishing third in total points behind teammates Ted Lindsay and Sid Abel. His Red Wings led the league standings and were favoured to oust Toronto in the first round of the playoffs.

But in the opening game of the playoffs, on March 28, 1950, the Wings almost lost their brilliant right winger forever. In the third period, with the Leafs in front 5–0, Toronto captain Ted Kennedy, leading a rush, was intercepted by Howe.

"I was going to run Kennedy into the boards," Howe recalled, "and was leaning in when Kennedy's stick came around and spiked me right in the eye. But the real shocker came a split second later, when I crashed into the boards."

Howe nosedived into the boards and collapsed to the ice, semi-conscious. Someone called for a stretcher and an ambulance. In the meantime, doctors and trainers diagnosed a broken nose, a possible broken cheekbone, damage to one eye, and a serious concussion.

"I'll never forget that horrible ride to the hospital," Howe has said. "I felt awful. Someone gave me a drink of water and I vomited. In the operating room, I remember them shaving my head."

A neurosurgeon drilled a small opening in Gordie's skull above his right ear to relieve the pressure on his brain. The surgeon would later say that if he had taken just 30 minutes longer to tend to Howe, the star could easily have lost his life.

Back at the Olympia, Kennedy was accused of deliberately butt-ending his opponent. Kennedy offered to swear an oath that he had not intended to harm Howe.

The Red Wings went on to eliminate the Leafs in a fight-filled series that ended with defenceman Leo Reise Jr.'s overtime winner in the seventh game. The Wings moved on to win the final series over the Rangers in seven games, with Pete Babando scoring the winner in double overtime. The crowd at the Olympia immediately began chanting, "We want Howe!" and moments later, Gordie emerged from the players' entrance, his head swathed in bandages. He received a tumultuous ovation, and with tears in his eyes, he reached out to touch the Stanley Cup.

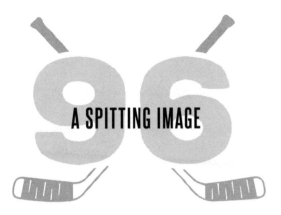

A SPITTING IMAGE

You may not remember Jack (better known as Jackie) Hamilton. The young man broke in as a 17-year-old with the Toronto Maple Leafs in 1942–43 — one of the youngest rookies in history. For many seasons, long after he retired, I played right wing for the Ontario NHL Oldtimers on a line centred by Hamilton, who played pro at 160 pounds and for the Oldtimers at 260. The weight slowed his skating just a tad and he disdained backchecking, leaving that to his wingers.

"You know how I won a few faceoffs in the NHL?" he said to me once. "I'd go to our bench and take a swig of water. But I wouldn't swallow. I'd lean in close to the opposing centre and just as the puck was dropped, I'd squirt water through my teeth into his face. He'd be left wiping water off his mug while I skated off with the puck. I got Milt Schmidt good with my water spray one time. True story."

He told me, "Here's another. Get this. I'm racing in on goal one night when a big fellow nailed me and flipped me high in the air. When I came down, my skate got caught in the chicken wire behind the net and I was left hanging there — upside down and helpless. I yelled at the goalie to come help me and he just laughed at me. I don't know how long I hung there, but finally there was a whistle and my mates came to rescue me. But the crowd loved it. Everybody was laughing — everybody but me."

TAKING THE GLOVES OFF

In the 1960s, Carl Brewer was a talented young defence-man for the Toronto Maple Leafs. Referee Vern Buffey in particular marvelled at the way Brewer played his position. Buffey could never figure out how Brewer could throw bigger men off balance and make them look like incompetent bumblers whenever they tried to outmuscle him.

One night there was a brawl in a Leafs game, and gloves and sticks were flung aside. When order was restored, Buffey noticed a very unusual hockey glove lying on the ice. He picked it up and found the glove had no palm. Why would a player cut the palm out of his glove, Buffey wondered? When Carl Brewer claimed the glove, Buffey figured it out.

In those goalmouth skirmishes, Brewer had been slipping his hands through the holes in his gloves and grabbing opponents by the sweater. He then tugged them backward or sideways and threw them off balance.

It was a neat trick, but Buffey's discovery of Brewer's modification led to a new NHL rule: No more palmless hockey gloves.

Carl Brewer was at his best when he threw off his gloves — holes and all — and in retirement, battled his former employers. In April 1991, he was among seven former players, including Gordie Howe and Bobby Hull, who filed a lawsuit in Canada against each NHL club and the NHL Pension Society, claiming the owners had misallocated surplus pension money in the millions.

In 1992, when a judge ruled in favour of the players, the NHL eventually reached a settlement with Brewer and friends to pay $40 million from surplus pension funds. That lawsuit ultimately led to criminal charges against Alan Eagleson, who served six months in prison for fraud and theft.

Brewer, often ripped for being a rebel, was suddenly every hockey player's pal — a hockey hero. He was definitely one of mine. Alas, he didn't get the chance to hear all of the plaudits. He died in his sleep in 2006 at the age of 62.

GADSBY HAD NO LUCK AT ALL

As a youth, Bill Gadsby recovered from polio, a disease that might have prevented him from a career in hockey. And when the ship he sailed on from England during the war went to the ocean floor, torpedoed by a German U-boat, young Gadsby and his mother were lucky to survive. But in the NHL, luck often deserted the all-star defenceman.

Gadsby played the first 15 years of his career with Chicago and New York, teams that made the playoffs a combined four times from 1946 to 1961. Only after the Rangers traded him to the Red Wings did he experience the joys of winning. The Wings breezed to the Cup Final in three of Gadsby's last five seasons. But he never got to taste champagne from Lord Stanley's old basin. Toronto swept the Wings aside in five games in 1963 and in seven games in 1964, with

Bobby Baun's overtime goal on a broken leg a factor in Game 6. "Bah," Gadsby often said. "His leg wasn't broken. He may have had a hairline fracture, but the media played it up big."

The following season, 1964–65, the Blackhawks ousted the Wings in seven games in the semifinals. "Bobby Hull and Glenn Hall did us in that year," recalls Gadsby. "By then I was almost 38 years old.

"In the '66 playoffs, we reached the finals against Montreal. The Habs were huge favourites. We played the first two games in Montreal, and Roger Crozier, our little goalie, just stoned them and we won both games.

"I really thought we had them and I'd finally sip from the Cup. But the Habs stormed back and won the next two back in Detroit. They won again in Montreal, and now we're back home for Game 6. Suddenly we're playin' great again and we're tied with the Canadiens after regulation time.

"Early in the overtime period, Henri Richard flew in on Crozier. Somehow Richard fell down and he's sliding toward our goal and the puck came to him and he slid with it under his arm all the way into our net. I saw him shove the damn thing in with his arm. I swear he did. But the red light flashed and the Habs began jumping on the ice. The series was over. We'd lost another chance at the Cup. I still can't believe it ended like it did.

"I'm sure that Montreal coach Toe Blake thought Richard's goal would be called back. The second the red light flashed, he yelled down the bench, 'Get out on the ice! Get out there!' So the Habs tumbled over the boards and headed for Richard. Toe didn't want to give the referee time to question the legality of the goal, nor time to confer with anyone else."

To the Habs, another Cup win was old hat. It was their seventh in the past 11 years. But to Gadsby, it was a tragedy, the end of his Stanley Cup dream.

A SAD END TO A BRILLIANT CAREER

December 12, 1933, was a tragic day in the history of NHL hockey. A crushing bodycheck delivered in anger — and from behind — by Bruins tough guy Eddie Shore ended Leafs star Irvine "Ace" Bailey's hockey career and left him near death with a fractured skull. (Bailey was not related to the Ace Bailey mentioned earlier in this book.)

In the second period of a Leafs-Bruins game, Eddie Shore made one of his flashy rushes and was tripped up by King Clancy at the Toronto blue line. Shore jumped to his feet and targeted the nearest Leaf for a return check. The innocent opponent was Bailey, who stood with his back to Shore.

Shore struck Bailey with his right shoulder, sending him into a backward somersault. Bailey's head hit the ice with terrific force, fracturing his skull in two places. An awestruck hush fell over the Boston Garden crowd.

Toronto's Red Horner, a muscular defenceman, made a beeline for Shore and poleaxed him with a right to the jaw. Shore collapsed to the ice.

Bailey and Shore were carried to their respective dressing rooms. Bailey then began convulsing and, barely conscious, was rushed to a Boston hospital. Two delicate brain operations in the next 10 days helped save his life. The Leafs forward never played hockey again, but he made a satisfactory recovery and lived to the age of 88.

Shore's head wound required several stitches. His reckless behaviour earned him a 16-game suspension.

Two months after the incident, in Toronto, a benefit game between the Bruins and the Leafs was held for Bailey, who bought a new house with the money raised. Bailey and Shore shook hands, and the Toronto fans roared their approval at the sportsmanship displayed.

A LOVER AND A FIGHTER

At the 1996 Hall of Fame induction ceremonies in Toronto, I asked Rod Gilbert if he would mind if I used a quote about him from one of his former girlfriends.

"What's the quote?" he asked.

"Well, it's the one an actress friend made many years ago, about you being the most fantastic lover she's ever had."

Rod's eyes lit up and he laughed. "Geez, use it!" he said. "Be sure and use it. It's a great quote. Hell, that's a lot better than being called a great hockey player."

During his Hall of Fame career, Gilbert survived two delicate back operations, as well as a blood clot (a complication from surgery) that could have cost him his life. When he had the blood clot, the surgeons conferred and debated whether or not to amputate his leg. "I was scared to death,"

Gilbert recalls. "Not only was my hockey career in doubt, but there was a chance I might leave the hospital with one leg missing — if I left at all."

Fortunately, the medics were able to dissolve the blood clot, and within days, Gilbert was able to start rehab.

Gilbert went under the knife for a second time on February 1, 1966. And he almost didn't survive. "I died on the operating table that day," he confided to me. "I was gone for maybe three or four minutes, and I left my body. It was an amazing experience. I looked down from above the table and I saw them working on me, trying to restore my heartbeat. Emile Francis [Rangers coach and GM] was there — why would he be in the room? When the nurse said, 'I think we've lost him,' Emile jumped up and shouted, 'You can't lose him. He's my best right winger. Bring him back!' And somehow, they brought me back."

FOX BEATS ORR TO SCORE!

In the late 1980s and through 1990, I enjoyed working on a feature for *Hockey Night in Canada* called "Inside Hockey," a three- to four-minute segment that ran during the second intermission. One I particularly enjoyed featured Canadian actor Michael J. Fox, who is a huge hockey fan. Fox grew up in Canada and played minor hockey in North Bay.

Michael said, "Brian, I had a chance to play a game against Bobby Orr in the Boston Garden — one of those Hollywood Legends games for charity. We played against Bobby and the Bruins, and what a thrill it was. It was a moment that you could not put a price tag on. It was amazing!

"This was all about Bobby Orr skating in the Boston Garden for the first time in many years. People didn't know whether Bobby would be able to skate again, and the ovation he received was just unbelievable. Apparently Bobby had to have more knee surgery following that game. But Bobby did it for the people of Boston.

"Get this. Before the game, Bobby came up to me … I couldn't speak. Now, I have met presidents and queens and all kinds of celebrities, and I try not to get flustered. But when Bobby spoke to me, I opened my mouth and couldn't speak. I didn't even know my name. I mean, it's Bobby Orr! Someone you looked up to your whole life.

"Bobby was saying to me, 'Michael, you pull the puck away from me at the blue line and break away and score.' I just nodded, and sure enough, in the first period, I steal the puck from Bobby. I just pushed it through his blades — that was easy — and now I'm past him. Well, I fall down and get back up and slap the puck in the upper corner of the net, and man, it felt cool.

"Well, the game's over and we're all having a beer and everybody's talking about my goal, when it dawns on me: Bobby had let me have the puck so that I could score. He not only proved that he was a greater hockey player than I could ever be in my whole life, he also proved that he was a better actor than I am. So, if people think I beat Bobby Orr at the blue line and went in and scored, well, that's fine with me. And if they ask Bobby about it, knowing him, he'll say, 'It's true. Mikey took the puck right off my stick, and he's so fast I couldn't catch up to him.'"

Brief Contents

Detailed Contents

**Part II   Information Gathering,
Analysis, and Manipulation   95**

Part V   Applications   391